ROTOGRAPHIC

Specialist publishers of price guide reference books. Established 1959

Check Your Change

By Chris Henry Perkins.

Important research and initial layout concept by Scott D Simon.

6th Edition © 2008

ISBN13: 978-0-948964-80-0

A comprehensive UK decimal coin and circulating banknote catalogue. Collectors' issues, Proof and BU sets plus Gold and Silver bullion issues are included.

Errors and Omissions:

Every effort has been made to ensure that the information and price data contained within this book are accurate and complete. However, errors do sometimes have a habit of creeping in unnoticed, and with this in mind the following email address has been established for notifications of ￼￼￼￼ info@rotographic.com Readers within the UK can also call the telephone number below

Rotographic Intern.
PO BOX 4943
London, SE20 7

www.rotographic.com
0871 871 5122

In Association with Predecimal

TABLE OF CONTENTS

INTRODUCTION

BACKGROUND OF DECIMALISATION

LISTINGS

INTRODUCTION

In the late 60s, when people knew that the old money would soon be replaced with decimal coins, everybody was checking their change for the first time. The original Rotographic 'Check Your Change' book sold 1.75 million copies back then.

Decimal coinage has been with us for forty years but is often overlooked as it has yet to prove itself in the test of time. As time progresses I believe that interest in decimal coinage will increase and with this new interest will come a need for reference material. This book is designed to begin the process of compiling in-depth records of the coinage minted by the Royal Mint and to (hopefully) become a fundamental reference guide for all decimal coinage.

The main aim of this book is to put the general public 'in the know' about the coins and banknotes that they handle every day - the scarce coin types and the banknotes with the rare serial numbers. As the title suggests, this is a guide book on how to 'Check Your Change'.

Rumours frequently do the rounds about this coin or that banknote being worth huge amounts of money. Mostly, these rumours are unfounded and all they do is annoy coin dealers who end up taking call upon call from soon-to-be disappointed people! This book contains the facts and no Chinese whispers.

I also believe that this inexpensive book, with listings and colour pictures of every single decimal coin type and circulating banknote, will provide an excellent guide to modern coinage and as such, should aid existing collectors and hopefully, stimulate new ones. This should hopefully lead to a wider collector base, and as a result, more business for coin dealers and banknote dealers across the country.

In short, it is time once again to 'Check Your Change'.
Be armed with the same information that coin collectors have had for years!

Good luck,
Chris Henry Perkins, London, January 2008.

NEW IN 2008

Probably the most interesting recent development for people that like to Check their Change is the issue by the Bank of England of £10 notes with Merlyn Lowther signatures and higher prefixes than was thought possible! Until recently it was thought that the Merlyn Lowther £10 notes with CC prefixes stopped at CC40 in 2003. The earliest CC prefixes from her successor are CC41. It seems though that the Bank must be using up old stocks of paper bearing the Lowther signature as crisp new notes with CC prefixes as high as CC77 have been seen for Lowther £10 notes. At the time of writing CC77 Lowther £10 notes have been selling for £50+ each as banknote collectors believe that they are the very last Lowther £10 notes. The fragile thing here is that as soon as CC78 appears (if it does) the CC77 notes are likely to be worth £10 again! No one knows how high the Bank of England will go with the Lowther CC prefix, and for obvious reasons they never make that kind of information available to the public. Will the old paper stock run out at CC77 or will it go right up to, or beyond CC80? I'd certainly like to here about any Lowther £10 notes with CC prefixes higher than CC77.

As far as coins are concerned, take a look at page 53 for details on a newly discovered £2 silver proof coin with an incorrect edge inscription. Page 55 features Britains only £2.50 coin!

USING THIS CATALOGUE

The values listed in this catalogue are the result of many hours of compiling and comparing the prices offered by online dealers, online auctions, dealer sales lists, live-auction catalogues, and other sources. For some items, there is such a limited number of transactions on which to base the values that they may seem conservative.

Values are only given for uncirculated grades at the current time. The reason for this decision is that with the high mintage figures of virtually all coins covered in this catalogue, any coin that is not in uncirculated grade usually has virtually no value above the face value. As a matter of fact, many recent issues are so readily available that even in uncirculated grades, they have no value above face value. (such coins are listed as FV - Face Value). Please remember: **Most modern coins are only desirable in UNC condition, which means 'as new'.**

It must also be realised that especially with the lower valued coins, the time and effort needed to document, catalogue, and list these items for sale by a dealer is often not cost-effective, and thus it is often much more difficult to locate a particular coin than the low value would indicate.

MINTAGES

The numbers given as mintages are based on information available from many sources, including other reference works, online sources, and the Royal Mint. The accuracy of these numbers is by no means guaranteed, and modifications may be made as better information becomes available.

It must also be noted that for the later issues, the mintages given are what are listed as the "maximum mintages", and the actual number of pieces struck may be currently unknown. Again, updates will be made as allowed.

COIN GRADES

The listings in this catalogue contain three prices, where applicable. The guidelines for these grades are as follows:

Uncirculated (UNC)
Appears as it did when it left the Mint. There will be no signs of wear or handling. May show "bag marks", as is common for mass-produced coins.

Brilliant uncirculated (BU)
A high end uncirculated. Fewer "bag marks" visible, most of the mint lustre remaining. Most coins from Specimen in folders or sealed packaging would be considered as BU.

Proof (PR)
A coin usually struck from specially prepared coin dies on a specially prepared metal blank. Proofs are usually given more than one blow from the dies and are usually struck with presses operating at slower speeds and higher striking pressures. Because of this extra care, Proofs usually exhibit much sharper detail than the regular coins, which are often called business strikes.

THE VALUE OF GOLD

At the time of writing this 2008 edition the price of gold on international markets is buoyant A short while ago it rose to over £400 per ounce and now over £450 per ounce. Such sharp increases sometimes loose their pace and can steady themselves at a lower limit. By the time this book goes to print the price of gold may have fallen again, or may have hit £500 per ounce! The price of gold influences the prices quoted in this book for gold coins, so it should be borne in mind that the gold coin prices quoted here are based on a price of about £457 per ounce (£14,700 per kilogramme).

THE DECIMALISATION OF UNITED KINGDOM COINAGE

Ever since the decimalisation of the French Franc in 1795, there was discussion and debate over the conversion of the British currency to a decimal standard. In 1849 the Victorians introduced the florin denomination which was worth two shillings, or one tenth of a pound. It was not until the conversion of the South African currency in 1960 that any serious consideration was given to a complete changeover. Following the report of the Halsbury Committee (Committee of the Enquiry on Decimal Currency) in 1963, and approval of the recommendations of the Committee in 1966, a Decimal Currency Board (DCB) was created to initiate and carry out the plans, approved by Parliament as the Decimal Currency Act of July 1967.

The decision was made to keep the pound sterling as the core unit of currency, and to divide it into 100 equal units, retaining the "penny" name, but adding the "new" to help distinguish the decimal system from the £.s.d. system. By using this system, the shilling (which was worth 1/20th of a pound), became the equivalent of the 5 new pence, and the florin (1/10th of a pound) became 10 new pence. This was a vital step in ensuring a smooth transition period, as the shilling and florin pieces remained in circulation for an extended period of time after "Decimalisation Day", which was the 15th of February 1971.

Several pre-decimal coins remained legally in circulation after "Decimalisation Day", including the florin and shilling mentioned above, along with the sixpence piece, which had a decimal value of 2½ new pence (thus requiring the issuance of a ½ new penny piece to accommodate its usage).

In 1972, the striking of decimal base-metal commemorative crowns began, with a value of 25 new pence, which is the equivalent of 5 shillings (the pre-decimal value of a "crown"). Four issues were minted between 1972 and 1981. In 1990 the base metal crown returned, again, but with a face value of £5. Although they are legal tender, they seldom see circulation.

In 1982 a 20p coin was introduced. Interestingly, the Victorian Double Florin coin, which was struck from 1887 to 1892, was not officially demonetised in 1971 (as far as the author can find out) so thoretically you could spend a Double Florin as a 20p coin. To actually do so would be quite silly because the silver content of the said Victorian coin is probably worth at least £9!

In 1983 a £1 coin was introduced, and the £1 Bank of England banknote was retired as a cost-cutting measure (Scottish banks continued issuing £1 notes). With the increased popularity and usage of the £1 coin, in 1997 a circulating £2 bi-metal coin was first struck.

TIMELINE OF DECIMAL COINAGE

1968	Introduction of new portrait of QEII, by Arnold Machin. 5 new pence (shilling-sized) & 10 new pence (florin-sized) are introduced.
1969	The 50 new pence coin is introduced, to replace the 10 shilling notes. Pre-decimal halfpennies and half-crowns are demonetised.
1971	The 15th of February 1971 is "Decimalisation Day." ½, 1 and 2 new pence are officially introduced (these were originally issued in 1968 & 1969 wallets). Pre-decimal pennies and threepence are demonetised. Proof sets of decimal coins are introduced.
1972	The first 25 pence commemorative crown is struck.
1973	The first 50 pence commemorative coin is struck.
1980	Pre-decimal sixpences are demonetised. The word "New" is dropped from all coinage.
1982	The 20 pence piece is introduced. BU Annual Royal Mint folders are introduced.
1983	£1 coins are introduced to replace the £1 note.
1984	½ pennies are demonetised.
1985	Introduction of new portrait of QEII, by Raphael Maklouf.
1986	The first commemorative £2 coin is struck.
1990	Pre-decimal post-1816 shillings and the large initial 5 pence are demonetised. At the same time a smaller 5 pence is introduced.
1990	The Crown is given a face value of £5 (instead of 25p) and the first commemorative £5 crown is struck.
1993	The 1p and 2p are changed from bronze to copper-plated steel.
1993	Pre-decimal florins and the large initial 10 pence are demonetised. At the same time a smaller 10 pence is introduced.
1997	New bi-metallic £2 coins are circulated.
1997	The new smaller 50 pence replaces the old large type.
1998	Introduction of the new portrait of Her Majesty the Queen, by Ian Rank-Broadley.
2008	Planned introduction of a complete range of new designs to be used on all British decimal coins.

What's currently legal tender?
No half pennies are legal tender any longer. They were demonetised on the 31st December 1984. Banks might accept them, but I shouldn't think the high street financial institutions would be falling over themselves to exchange the half-pee tiddlers!

Which are hard to find?
The 1972 coin was made as a proof only and went into sets, so is harder to find. The last coin, dated 1984, was only made for sets only, so is also harder to find.

OBVERSE

OBVERSE 1
(used 1971 - 1984)
D•G•REG•F•D•(date) | | ELIZABETH II
Elizabeth II, Dei Gratia Regina, Fidei Defensor
(Elizabeth II, By the Grace of God Queen and Defender of the Faith)
Portrait by: Arnold Machin

REVERSE

REVERSE 1
(used 1971 - 1981)
Regal Crown
½ NEW PENNY
Design by: Christopher Ironside

REVERSE 2
(used 1982 - 1984)
Regal Crown
½ HALF PENNY
Design by: Christopher Ironside

INFO
Although it was known from the onset that the half-penny would see limited circulation, it was necessary to help facilitate the transition from the Sterling standard to decimal, as the old sixpence pieces were still circulating as 2½ new pence.

TYPE 1 (obverse 1, reverse 1)

			UNC	BU	Proof
1971	1,394,188,250		£0.05	£0.10	£2.00
1972		Proof Only			£5.00
1973	365,680,000		£0.10	£0.20	£2.00
1974	365,448,000		£0.10	£0.20	£2.00
1975	197,600,000		£0.10	£0.20	£2.00
1976	412,172,000		£0.10	£0.20	£2.00
1977			£0.10	£0.20	£2.00
1978	59,532,000		£0.10	£0.20	£2.00
1979			£0.10	£0.20	£2.00
1980			£0.10	£0.20	£2.00
1981	46,748,000		£0.10	£0.20	£2.00

TYPE 2 (obverse 1, reverse 2)

			UNC	BU	Proof
1982	190,752,000		£0.05	£0.10	£2.00
1983	7,600,000		£0.10	£0.20	£2.00
1984	158,820	[2]	£2.00	£2.00	£3.00

DOCUMENTED ERRORS
1971 double-headed (minting error) £200

NOTES
[1]   Each year, it is determined, based upon supply and demand, what denominations will be struck for circulation. These years were not issued for circulation, and no "business strikes" were made.
[2]   These years were not issued for circulation, and the "business strikes" were made for BU mint folders, only.

What's currently legal tender?
All 1p coins are legal tender. Merchants are allowed by law to refuse payments made in 1p or 2p coins if the combined value of the 'coppers' is more than 20p in any one transaction.

Which are hard to find?
The 1972 coin was made as a proof only and went into sets, so is not likely to be found in circulation. In 1992 the Royal Mint changed from using bronze to using copper-plated steel. In that year both types exist and the bronze 1992 is not usually found in circulation.

There is no 'NEW PENNY' error coin relating to one pennies. All 1971 to 1981 coins have 'NEW PENNY' on the reverse and all 1982 to date coins have 'ONE PENNY' on the reverse.... at least they should do! So far no errors have been reported.

OBVERSE

OBVERSE 1
(used 1971 - 1984)
D•G•REG•F•D•(date) | | ELIZABETH II
Elizabeth II, Dei Gratia Regina, Fidei Defensor
(Elizabeth II, By the Grace of God Queen and Defender of the Faith)
Portrait by: Arnold Machin

OBVERSE 2
(used 1985 - 1997)
ELIZABETH II | | D•G•REG•F•D•(date)
Elizabeth II, Dei Gratia Regina, Fidei Defensor
(Elizabeth II, By the Grace of God Queen and Defender of the Faith)
Portrait by: Raphael Maklouf

OBVERSE 3
(used 1998 to date)
ELIZABETH•II•D•G | | REG•F•D•(date)
Elizabeth II, Dei Gratia Regina, Fidei Defensor
(Elizabeth II, By the Grace of God Queen and Defender of the Faith)
Portrait by: Ian Rank–Broadley

REVERSE

REVERSE 1
(used 1971 - 1981)
Crowned portcullis
[OFFICIALLY: A portcullis with chains
royally crowned]
1 NEW PENNY
Design by: Christopher Ironside

REVERSE 2
(used 1982 to date)
Crowned portcullis
[OFFICIALLY: A portcullis with chains
royally crowned]
1 ONE PENNY
Design by: Christopher Ironside

TYPE 1 (obverse 1, reverse 1)

		UNC	BU	Proof
1971	1,521,666,250	£0.05	£0.10	£2.00
1972	Proof Only			£5.00
1973	280,196,000	£0.20	£1.00	£3.00
1974	330,892,000	£0.20	£1.00	£3.00
1975	221,604,000	£0.20	£1.00	£3.00
1976	241,800,000	£0.20	£1.00	£3.00
1977	285,430,000	£0.20	£1.00	£3.00
1978	292,770,000	£0.20	£1.00	£2.00
1979	459,000,000	£0.20	£1.00	£2.00
1980	416,304,000	£0.20	£1.00	£2.00
1981	301,800,000	£0.20	£1.00	£2.00

TYPE 2 (obverse 1, reverse 2)

		UNC	BU	Proof
1982	100,292,000	£0.20	£0.70	£2.00
1983	243,002,000	£0.20	£0.70	£2.00
1984	154,759,625	£0.20	£0.70	£2.00

20.32 mm • 3.56 grammes • bronze • plain edge

TYPE 3 (obverse 2, reverse 2)

			UNC	BU	Proof
1985	200,605,245		£0.05	£0.70	£2.00
1986	369,989,130		£0.05	£0.70	£2.00
1987	499,946,000		£0.05	£0.70	£2.00
1988	793,492,000		£0.05	£0.70	£2.00
1989	658,142,000		£0.05	£0.70	£2.00
1990	529,047,500		£0.05	£0.70	£2.00
1991	206,457,600		£0.05	£0.70	£2.00
1992	78,421 ‡AI	Bronze	£3.00	£3.00	£3.00

TYPE 4 (obverse 2, reverse 2)
From now on made of copper-plated steel (slightly magnetic)

		UNC	BU	Proof
1992	253,867,000	FV	£0.10	...
1993	602,590,000	FV	£0.10	£2.00
1994	843,834,000	FV	£0.10	£2.00
1995	303,314,000	FV	£0.10	£2.00
1996	723,840,060	FV	£0.10	£2.00
1997	396,874,000	FV	£0.10	£2.00

TYPE 5 (obverse 3, reverse 2)

		UNC	BU	Proof
1998	739,770,000	FV	£0.05	£2.00
1999	891,392,000	FV	£0.05	£2.00
2000		FV	£0.05	£2.00
2001		FV	FV	£2.00
2002		FV	FV	£2.00
2003		FV	FV	£2.00
2004		FV	FV	£2.00
2005		FV	FV	£2.00
2006		FV	FV	£2.00
2007		FV	FV	£2.00

NOTES

‡1 These years were not issued for circulation, and no "business strikes" were made.

‡2 These years were not issued for circulation, and the "business strikes" were made for BU mint folders, only.

‡AI In 1992, a change in materials was made from bronze to copper-plated steel. In 1992 the original bronze planchets were only used for the BU Mint folders and Proof sets. The copper-plated steel planchets were used for circulation strikes only.

What's currently legal tender?
All 2p coins are legal tender.

Which are hard to find?
The change from using bronze to using copper-plated steel has led to a couple of scarcer types. The 1992 coin made of bronze (i.e. not magnetic) is much scarcer than the 1992 coin made of copper-plated steel. The same kind of thing happened in 1998.

By far the rarest and most expensive 2p is the 1983 error coin, which has NEW PENCE on the back instead of TWO PENCE. This mistake just affects the 1983 2p; no other coins have been noted with this error. The error coins went into sets and were not generally circulated. It is possible though, that some of the sets were broken up before the error was noticed, so there may be a few £500 2p coins out there somewhere!

OBVERSE

OBVERSE 1
(used 1971 - 1984)
D•G•REG•F•D•(date) || ELIZABETH II
Elizabeth II, Dei Gratia Regina, Fidei Defensor
(Elizabeth II, By the Grace of God Queen and Defender of the Faith)
Portrait by: Arnold Machin

OBVERSE 2
(used 1985 - 1997)
ELIZABETH II || D•G•REG•F•D•(date)
Elizabeth II, Dei Gratia Regina, Fidei Defensor
(Elizabeth II, By the Grace of God Queen and Defender of the Faith)
Portrait by: Raphael Maklouf

OBVERSE 3
(used 1998 to date)
ELIZABETH•II•D•G || REG•F•D•(date)
Elizabeth II, Dei Gratia Regina, Fidei Defensor
(Elizabeth II, By the Grace of God Queen and Defender of the Faith)
Portrait by: Ian Rank–Broadley

REVERSES

REVERSE 1
(used 1971 - 1981)
Plumes in Coronet
[OFFICIALLY: The Badge of the Prince of Wales, with its motto ICH DIEN]
2 NEW PENCE
Design by: Christopher Ironside

13

25.91 mm • 7.13 grammes • bronze • plain edge

REVERSE 2
(used 1982 to date)
Plumes in Coronet
[OFFICIALLY: The Badge of the Prince of
Wales, with its motto ICH DIEN]
2 TWO PENCE
Design by: Christopher Ironside

TYPE 1 (obverse 1, reverse 1)

	UNC	BU	Proof
1971	£0.05	£0.10	£2.00
1972 Proof Only [#1]			£4.00
1973 Proof Only [#1]			£4.00
1974 Proof Only [#1]			£4.00
1975	£0.10	£0.25	£2.00
1976	£0.10	£0.25	£2.00
1977	£0.10	£0.25	£2.00
1978	£0.10	£0.25	£2.00
1979	£0.10	£0.25	£2.00
1980	£0.10	£0.25	£2.00
1981	£0.10	£0.25	£2.00

TYPE 2 (obverse 1, reverse 2)

		UNC	BU	Proof
1982	205,000 [+2]	£2.00	£2.00	£2.00
1983	631,000 [+2]	£2.00	£2.00	£2.00
1983	Not Known Error, NEW PENCE reverse	£500.00		
1984	158,820 [+2]	£2.00	£2.00	£2.00

TYPE 3 (obverse 2, reverse 2)

		UNC	BU	Proof
1985	107,113,000	£0.10	£0.25	£2.00
1986	168,967,500	£0.10	£0.25	£2.00
1987	218,100,750	£0.10	£0.25	£2.00
1988	419,889,000	£0.10	£0.25	£2.00
1989	359,226,000	£0.10	£0.25	£2.00
1990	204,499,700	£0.10	£0.25	£2.00
1991	86,625,000	£0.10	£0.25	£2.00
1992	78,421 [+B1] Bronze	£3.00	£3.00	£3.00

TYPE 4 (obverse 2, reverse 2)
From now on made of copper-plated steel (slightly magnetic)

			UNC	BU	Proof
1992	102,247,000		£0.05	£0.10	-
1993	235,674,000		£0.05	£0.10	£2.00
1994	531,628,000		£0.05	£0.10	£2.00
1995	124,482,000		£0.05	£0.10	£2.00
1996	296,276,000		£0.05	£0.10	£2.00
1997	496,116,000		£0.05	£0.10	£2.00

TYPE 5 (obverse 3, reverse 2)

			UNC	BU	Proof
1998	231,830,000	Copper / Steel	FV	£0.05	£2.00
1998	About 55% of total [B2]	Bronze	FV	£0.05	
1999	353,816,000	Copper / Steel	FV	£0.05	£2.00
1999	[B3]	Bronze Proof			£3.00
2000	583,643,000		FV	£0.05	£2.00
2001	551,886,000		FV	FV	£2.00
2002	168,556,000		FV	FV	£2.00
2003	248,710,000		FV	FV	£2.00
2004			FV	FV	£2.00
2005			FV	FV	£2.00
2006			FV	FV	£2.00
2007			FV	FV	£2.00

NOTES

[1] These years were not issued for circulation, and no "business strikes" were made.

[2] These years were not issued for circulation, and the "business strikes" were made for BU mint folders, only.

[B1] In 1992, a change in materials was made from bronze to copper-plated steel. The original bronze blanks were only used for the BU Mint folders and Proof sets. The copper-plated steel blanks were used for circulation strikes, only.

[B2] In 1998, both bronze and copper-plated steel blanks were used. It is estimated that about 55% of the mintage was bronze.

[B3] In 1999, bronze blanks were used for Proof sets.

INFO

The current minting facility at Llantrisant, Mid Glamorgan, was built in 1967, in order to meet the demand for the millions of coins needed for the conversion to the modern decimal system used in the United Kingdom.

15

What's currently legal tender?

Only the smaller post-1990 5p coins are legal tender. The older large coins can be paid into most UK bank accounts. The predecessor of the five pence, the shilling, should also be accepted at most UK banks as five pence. Obviously, check the shillings have no collectable worth using the Roto-graphic Publication "Collectors' Coins Great Britain" before redeeming them as five pences!

Which are hard to find?

The old large 5p coins are no longer found in change (unless someone has managed to pass one off as a 10p, which sometimes happens). The scarcest are those that were made just to go into sets, or as proofs: notably 1972 to 1974, 1976, a few of the early and mid 1980s coins, and the last large 5p struck in 1990.

OBVERSE

OBVERSE 1
(used 1971 - 1984)
D•G•REG•F•D•(date) || ELIZABETH II
Elizabeth II, Dei Gratia Regina, Fidei Defensor
(Elizabeth II, By the Grace of God Queen and Defender of the Faith)
Portrait by: Arnold Machin

OBVERSE 2
(used 1985 - 1990)
ELIZABETH II || D•G•REG•F•D•(date)
Elizabeth II, Dei Gratia Regina, Fidei Defensor
(Elizabeth II, By the Grace of God Queen and Defender of the Faith)
Portrait by: Raphael Maklouf

REVERSE

REVERSE 1
(used 1971 - 1981)
Crowned Thistle
[OFFICIALLY: The Badge of Scotland, a thistle royally crowned]
5 NEW PENCE
Design by: Christopher Ironside

REVERSE 2
(used 1982 - 1990)
Crowned Thistle
[OFFICIALLY: The Badge of Scotland, a thistle royally crowned]
5 FIVE PENCE
Design by: Christopher Ironside

TYPE 1 (obverse 1, reverse 1)

		UNC	BU	Proof
1968	98,868,250	£0.08	£0.20	
1969	120,270,000	£0.10	£0.30	
1970	225,948,525	£0.10	£0.30	
1971	81,783,475	£0.10	£0.30	£2.00
1972	‡1			£5.00
1973	‡1			£5.00
1974	‡1			£5.00
1975	141,539,000	£0.20	£0.30	£2.00
1976	‡1			£2.00
1977	24,308,000	£0.20	£0.30	£2.00
1978	61,094,000	£0.20	£0.30	£2.00
1979	155,456,000	£0.20	£0.30	£2.00
1980	220,566,000	£0.20	£0.30	£2.00
1981	‡1			£3.00

TYPE 2 (obverse 1, reverse 2)

		UNC	BU	Proof
1982	205,000 ‡2	£3.00	£3.00	£3.00
1983	631,000 ‡2	£3.00	£3.00	£3.00
1984	158,820 ‡2	£3.00	£3.00	£3.00

TYPE 3 (obverse 2, reverse 2)

		UNC	BU	Proof
1985	178,000 ‡2	£3.00	£3.00	£3.00
1986	167,000 ‡2	£3.00	£3.00	£3.00
1987	48,220,000	£0.10	£0.30	£2.00
1988	120,744,610	£0.10	£0.30	£2.00
1989	101,406,000	£0.10	£0.25	£2.00
1990	102,606 ‡2	£2.00	£2.00	£2.00

NOTES
‡1   These years were not issued for circulation, and no "business strikes" were made.
‡2   These years were not issued for circulation, and the "business strikes" were made for BU mint folders, only.

18.0 mm • 7.13 grammes • cupro-nickel • milled edge

OBVERSE

OBVERSE 3
(used 1990 - 1997)
ELIZABETH II || D•G•REG•F•D•(date)
Elizabeth II, Dei Gratia Regina, Fidei Defensor
(Elizabeth II, By the Grace of God Queen and Defender of the Faith)
Portrait by: Raphael Maklouf

OBVERSE 4
(used 1998 to date)
ELIZABETH II•D•G || REG•F•D•(date)
Elizabeth II, Dei Gratia Regina, Fidei Defensor
(Elizabeth II, By the Grace of God Queen and Defender of the Faith)
Portrait by: Ian Rank–Broadley

REVERSE

REVERSE 3
(used 1990 to date)
Crowned Thistle
[OFFICIALLY: The Badge of Scotland, a thistle royally crowned]
5 FIVE PENCE
Design by: Christopher Ironside

INFO

As of December 31st 1990, the large five-pence coins were demonetised.

TYPE 4 (obverse 3, reverse 3)

			UNC	BU	Proof
1990	1,634,976,005		£0.05	£0.20	£2.00
1991	724,979,000		£0.05	£0.20	£2.00
1992	453,173,500		£0.05	£0.20	£2.00
1993	56,945 ‡2		£1.00	£1.00	£2.00
1994	93,602,000		£0.05	£0.20	£2.00
1995	183,384,000		£0.05	£0.20	£2.00
1996	302,902,000		£0.05	£0.20	£2.00
1997	736,596,000		£0.05	£0.15	£2.00

TYPE 5 (obverse 4, reverse 3)

			UNC	BU	Proof
1998	217,376,000	100,000 proofs	FV	£0.10	£2.00
1999	195,490,000		FV	£0.10	£2.00
2000	388,506,000		FV	£0.10	£2.00
2001	320,330,000		FV	FV	£2.00
2002	219,258,000		FV	FV	£2.00
2003	262,414,000		FV	FV	£2.00
2004	222,606,000		FV	FV	£2.00
2005			FV	FV	£2.00
2006			FV	FV	£2.00
2007			FV	FV	£2.00

NOTES

‡2   1993 was not issued for circulation, and the "business strikes" were made for BU mint folders, only.

What's currently legal tender?

Only the smaller post-1992 10p coins are legal tender. The older large coins can be paid into most UK bank account.s The predecessor of the ten pence, the florin, should also be accepted at most UK banks. Obviously, check the florins have no collectable worth using the Rotographic Publication "Collectors' Coins Great Britain" before redeeming them as ten pences!

Which are hard to find?

The old large 10p coins are no longer found in change. The scarcest are those that were made just to go into sets, or as proofs: notably 1972, 1978 and all of the large type coins from 1982 onwards.

OBVERSE

OBVERSE 1
(used 1971 - 1984)
D•G•REG•F•D•(date) || ELIZABETH II
Elizabeth II, Dei Gratia Regina, Fidei Defensor
(Elizabeth II, By the Grace of God Queen and Defender of the Faith)
Portrait by: Arnold Machin

OBVERSE 2
(used 1985 - 1992)
ELIZABETH II || D•G•REG•F•D•(date)
Elizabeth II, Dei Gratia Regina, Fidei Defensor
(Elizabeth II, By the Grace of God Queen and Defender of the Faith)
Portrait by: Raphael Maklouf

REVERSE

REVERSE 1
(used 1971 - 1981)
Lion Passant Guardant
[Part of the crest of England, a lion passant guardant royally crowned]
10 NEW PENCE
Design by: Christopher Ironside

REVERSE 2
(used 1982 - 1992)
Lion Passant Guardant
[Part of the crest of England, a lion passant guardant royally crowned]
10 TEN PENCE
Design by: Christopher Ironside

20

TYPE 1 (obverse 1, reverse 1)

		UNC	BU	Proof
1968	336,143,250	£0.15	£0.20	
1969	314,008,000	£0.15	£0.30	
1970	133,571,000	£0.15	£0.30	
1971	63,205,000	£0.15	£0.30	£2.00
1972	‡1 Proof Only			£2.00
1973	152,174,000	£0.15	£0.30	£2.00
1974	92,741,000	£0.15	£0.30	£2.00
1975	181,559,000	£0.15	£0.30	£2.00
1976	228,220,000	£0.15	£0.30	£2.00
1977	59,323,000	£0.15	£0.30	£2.00
1978	‡1 Proof Only			£2.00
1979	115,457,000	£0.15	£0.30	£2.00
1980	88,650,000	£0.20	£0.50	£2.00
1981	3,487,000	£1.00	£4.00	£7.00

TYPE 2 (obverse 1, reverse 2)

		UNC	BU	Proof
1982	205,000 ‡2	£3.00	£3.00	£3.00
1983	631,000 ‡2	£3.00	£3.00	£3.00
1984	158,820 ‡2	£3.00	£3.00	£3.00

TYPE 3 (obverse 2, reverse 2)

		UNC	BU	Proof
1985	178,000 ‡2	£3.00	£3.00	£3.00
1986	167,000 ‡2	£3.00	£3.00	£3.00
1987	172,425 ‡2	£3.00	£3.00	£2.00
1988	134,067 ‡2	£3.00	£3.00	£2.00
1989	77,569 ‡2	£3.00	£3.00	£2.00
1990	102,606 ‡2	£2.00	£3.00	£2.00
1991	74,975 ‡2	£2.00	£2.00	£2.00
1992	78,421 ‡2	£2.00	£2.00	£2.00

NOTES

‡1   These years were not issued for circulation, and no "business strikes" were made.

‡2   These years were not issued for circulation, and the "business strikes" were made for BU mint folders, only.

INFO

As of 30th June 1993, the large ten-pence coins were demonetised.

21

	24.50 mm • 6.5 grammes • cupro-nickel • milled edge

OBVERSE

OBVERSE 3
(used 1992 - 1997)
ELIZABETH II || D•G•REG•F•D•(date)
Elizabeth II, Dei Gratia Regina, Fidei Defensor
(Elizabeth II, By the Grace of God Queen and Defender of the Faith)
Portrait by: Raphael Maklouf

OBVERSE 4
(used 1998 -)
ELIZABETH II•D•G || REG•F•D•(date)
Elizabeth II, Dei Gratia Regina, Fidei Defensor
(Elizabeth II, By the Grace of God Queen and Defender of the Faith)
Portrait by: Ian Rank-Broadley

REVERSE

REVERSE 3
(used 1992 to date)
Lion Passant Guardant
[Part of the crest of England, a lion passant guardant royally crowned]
10 TEN PENCE
Design by: Christopher Ironside

TYPE 4 (obverse 3, reverse 3)

			UNC	BU	Proof
1992	1,413,455,170		£0.15	£0.20	£2.00
1993		‡Cl	£0.15	£0.20	£2.00
1994	56,945	‡2	£1.00	£2.00	£2.00
1995		‡2	£1.00	£2.00	£2.00
1996	43,259,000		£0.15	£0.20	£2.00
1997	118,738,000		£0.15	£0.20	£2.00

TYPE 5 (obverse 4, reverse 3)

			UNC	BU	Proof
1998		‡2 100,000 proofs	£2.00	£3.00	£2.00
1999		‡2	£2.00	£3.00	£2.00
2000	134,727,000		£0.15	£0.20	£2.00
2001	82,081,000		FV	FV	£2.00
2002	80,934,000		FV	FV	£2.00
2003	69,507,000		FV	FV	£2.00
2004			FV	FV	£2.00
2005		‡Cl	FV	FV	£2.00
2006		‡Cl	FV	FV	£2.00
2007			FV	FV	£2.00

NOTES

‡2   These years were not issued for circulation, and the "business strikes" were made for BU mint folders, only.

‡C1   Varieties exist for the 1992 issue, see below. Reverses 1 & 2 listed below have also been observed on 2005 and 2006 dated coins. It is not yet clear if one type is scarcer than the other.

TEN PENCE VARIETIES

The production of the new, smaller sized ten pence piece has yielded several varieties, some of which appear to be much less common than others.

The first type of ten pence pieces have a "wired" edge (left coin in both images), which has a curved edge, while all other varieties have a "flat" sharper edge (right coin in both images).

Obverse 1: The letters L and I in ELIZABETH point between 2 border beads. Obverse 2: The letters L and I in ELIZABETH point directly at border beads.

Reverse 1: The number 1 in the "10" points directly at a border bead. Reverse 2: The number 1 in the "10" points between 2 border beads.

TYPE 1: wired edge, obverse 1 reverse 1
Earliest type. It appears that the "wired" edge was abandoned sometime around midway through 1992 production. Represents approximately 40% of total mintage.

TYPE 2: flat edge, obverse 1 reverse 1
A continuation of the TYPE 1, but on different planchets with flat edges. This type also represents approximately 40% of the total mintage.

TYPE 3: flat edge, obverse 1 reverse 2
An extremely uncommon variety, referred to as the "between/between" type. Represents about 3% of the total mintage, perhaps a little less. This type could become desirable in the future.

TYPE 4: flat edge, obverse 2 reverse 1
The rarest variety, referred to as the "to dot/to dot" variety. Represents less than 1% of the total mintage, with some estimates as low as one half of 1%. This type may be worth saving for the future.

TYPE 5: flat edge, obverse 2 reverse 2
This type exhibits a new obverse and reverse style. Represents approximately 15% of the total mintage. This is the type is found in Proof sets and BU Mint folders.

What's currently legal tender?
All 20p coins are legal tender.

Victorian Double Florins also appear to be legal tender for 20p (4 shillings) as the author is unable to find any evidence that they were demonetised in 1971 with the rest of the old denominations. To spend one would be quite silly though, as the value of the silver contained within a double florin is far higher than 20p!

Which are hard to find?
The 1986 20p was made to be put in sets only and is therefore incredibly hard to find in change.

OBVERSE

OBVERSE 1
(used 1982 - 1984)
ELIZABETH II || D•G•REG•F•D
Elizabeth II, Dei Gratia Regina, Fidei Defensor
(Elizabeth II, By the Grace of God Queen and Defender of the Faith)
Portrait by: Arnold Machin

OBVERSE 2
(used 1985 - 1997)
ELIZABETH II || D•G•REG•F•D
Elizabeth II, Dei Gratia Regina, Fidei Defensor
(Elizabeth II, By the Grace of God Queen and Defender of the Faith)
Portrait by: Raphael Maklouf

OBVERSE 3
(used 1998 to date)
ELIZABETH II || D•G•REG•F•D
Elizabeth II, Dei Gratia Regina, Fidei Defensor
(Elizabeth II, By the Grace of God Queen and Defender of the Faith)
Portrait by: Ian Rank–Broadley

REVERSE

REVERSE 1
(used 1982 to date)
Crowned Tudor Rose
[The Badge of England, a royally crowned double rose]
20 TWENTY PENCE (date)
Design by: William Gardner

TYPE 1 (obverse 1, reverse 1)

		UNC	BU	Proof
1982	740,815,000	£0.30	£0.40	£2.00
	Specimen in folder		£6.00	
1983	158,463,000	£0.30	£0.40	£2.00
1984	65,350,965	£0.30	£0.40	£2.00

TYPE 2 (obverse 2, reverse 1)

		UNC	BU	Proof
1985	74,273,699	£0.30	£0.40	£2.00
1986	167,000 ‡2	£1.00	£3.00	£2.00
1987	137,450,000	£0.30	£0.40	£2.00
1988	38,038,344	£0.30	£0.40	£2.00
1989	132,013,890	£0.30	£0.40	£2.00
1990	88,097,500	£0.30	£0.40	£2.00
1991	35,901,250	£0.30	£0.40	£2.00
1992	31,205,000	£0.30	£0.50	£2.00
1993	123,123,750	£0.30	£0.50	£3.00
1994	67,131,250	£0.30	£0.50	£3.00
1995	102,005,000	£0.30	£0.50	£3.00
1996	83,163,750	£0.30	£0.50	£3.00
1997	89,518,750	£0.30	£0.50	£3.00

TYPE 3 (obverse 3, reverse 1)

		UNC	BU	Proof
1998	76,965,000	FV	£0.30	£3.00
1999	73,478,750	FV	£0.30	£3.00
2000		FV	FV	£2.00
2001		FV	FV	£2.00
2002		FV	FV	£2.00
2003		FV	FV	£2.00
2004		FV	FV	£2.00
2005		FV	FV	£2.00
2006		FV	FV	£2.00
2007		FV	FV	£2.00

NOTES

‡2   Each year, it is determined, based upon supply and demand, what denominations will be struck for circulation. 1986 was not issued for circulation, and the "business strikes" were made for BU mint folders, only.

Historically the Crown is five shillings (one quarter of a 20 shilling pound). Therefore these new decimal crowns have a face value of 25p. These four commemorative crown coins are legal tender for 25p, but they are rarely used by the public, probably because they are too big to be convenient, and to collectors they are usually worth a little more than face value. Members of the public often assume incorrectly that these four coins have a face value of £5, due to the fact that the crown was re-valued to £5 in 1990 although the size of the coin remained the same.

These four coins were issued to mark the following occasions: 1972 – The 25th Wedding Anniversary of the Queen and Prince Philip. 1977 - The Silver Jubilee of the Queen. 1980 - The 80th Birthday of the Queen Mother. 1981 - The Royal Wedding of Charles and Diana.

COMMEMORATIVE TYPE 1
Obverse: Standard portrait of QE II
Design by: Arnold Machin

Reverse: Elizabeth and Philip,
20 November 1947-1972
Design by: Arnold Machin

		UNC	BU	Proof
1972	7,452,100	£1.00	£2.00	£4.00
	100,000	.925 sterling silver cased proof		£24.00

COMMEMORATIVE TYPE 2
Obverse: Equestrian portrait of QE II
Design by: Arnold Machin

Reverse: Ampulla and anointing spoon,
items used during the Coronation
Design by: Arnold Machin

			UNC	BU	Proof
1977	37,061,160		£1.00	£2.00	£4.00
	Specimen in folder			£4.00	
	377,000	.925 sterling silver cased proof			£20.00

COMMEMORATIVE TYPE 3
Obverse: Standard portrait of QE II
Design by: Arnold Machin

Reverse: Portrait of Queen Mother,
surrounded by bows and lions
Design by: Richard Guyatt

			UNC	BU	Proof
1980	9,306,000	-	£1.00	£2.00	-
	Specimen in folder			£4.00	
	83,672	.925 sterling silver cased proof			£30.00

COMMEMORATIVE TYPE 4
Obverse: Standard portrait of QE II
Design by: Arnold Machin

Reverse: Conjoined busts of
Charles & Diana
Design by: Philip Nathan

			UNC	BU	Proof
1981	26,773,600	-	£1.00	£2.00	-
	Specimen in folder			£4.00	
	218,000	.925 sterling silver cased proof			£30.00

Set of 4 (72, 77, 80 and 81) Crowns as silver proofs in large case. 5000 sets issued   £55.00

27

30 mm • 13.5 grammes • cupro-nickel • plain edge

What's currently legal tender?
Only the smaller (post-1997) 50p coins are legal tender now. Most banks will allow you to pay in the pre-1997 larger 30mm coins.

Which are hard to find?
The larger pre-1997 coins are now rarely found in circulation. Many of the larger type coins have quite low mintages as they were either only made as proofs or as special BU strikings for the sets, and were not generally circulated.

OBVERSE

OBVERSE 1
(used 1969 - 1972, 1974 - 1984)
D•G•REG•F•D•(date) || ELIZABETH II
Elizabeth II, Dei Gratia Regina, Fidei Defensor
(Elizabeth II, By the Grace of God Queen and Defender of the Faith)
Portrait by: Arnold Machin

OBVERSE 2
(used 1985 - 1997)
ELIZABETH II || D•G•REG•F•D•(date)
Elizabeth II, Dei Gratia Regina, Fidei Defensor
(Elizabeth II, By the Grace of God Queen and Defender of the Faith)
Portrait by: Raphael Maklouf

REVERSE

REVERSE 1
(used 1969 - 1972, 1974 - 1981)
Britannia
[The seated figure of Britannia]
50 NEW PENCE
Design by: Christopher Ironside

REVERSE 2
(used 1982 - 93, 1995 - 1997)
Britannia
[The seated figure of Britannia]
50 FIFTY PENCE
Design by: Christopher Ironside

Britannia - TYPE 1 (obverse 1, reverse 1)

			UNC	BU	Proof
1969	188,400,000		£0.80	£2.00	
1970	19,461,500		£1.00	£3.00	
1971	‡1	Proof Only			£4.00
1972	‡1	Proof Only			£4.00
1974	‡1	Proof Only			£4.00
1975	‡1	Proof Only			£4.00
1976	43,746,500		£0.80	£2.00	£3.00
1977	49,536,000		£0.80	£2.00	£3.00
1978	72,005,500		£0.80	£2.00	£3.00
1979	58,680,000		£0.80	£2.00	£3.00
1980	89,086,000		£0.80	£2.00	£3.00
1981	74,002,000		£0.80	£2.00	£3.00

Britannia - TYPE 2 (obverse 1, reverse 2)

		UNC	BU	Proof
1982	51,312,000	£0.80	£2.00	£3.00
1983	62,824,904	£0.80	£2.00	£3.00
1984	158,820 ‡2	£2.00	£2.00	£3.00

Britannia - TYPE 3 (obverse 2, reverse 2)

		UNC	BU	Proof
1985	682,103	£1.00	£2.00	£3.00
1986	167,000 ‡2	£2.00	£2.00	£3.00
1987	172,425 ‡2	£2.00	£2.00	£3.00
1988	134,067 ‡2	£2.00	£2.00	£3.00
1989	77,569 ‡2	£2.00	£2.00	£3.00
1990	102,606 ‡2	£2.00	£2.00	£3.00
1991	74,975 ‡2	£2.00	£2.00	£3.00
1992	78,421 ‡2	£2.00	£2.00	£3.00
1993	56,945 ‡2	£2.00	£2.00	£3.00
1995	105,647 ‡2	£2.00	£2.00	£3.00
1996	86,501 ‡2	£2.00	£2.00	£3.00
1997	‡2	£2.00	£2.00	£3.00

NOTES

‡1   These years were not issued for circulation, and no "business strikes" were made.

‡2   These years were not issued for circulation, and the "business strikes" were made for BU mint folders, only.

27.3 mm • 8.0 grammes • cupro-nickel • plain edge

OBVERSE

OBVERSE 3
(used 1997)
ELIZABETH II | | D•G•REG•F•D•(date)
Elizabeth II, Dei Gratia Regina, Fidei Defensor
(Elizabeth II, By the Grace of God Queen and Defender of the Faith)
Portrait by: Raphael Maklouf

OBVERSE 4
(used 1998 to date)
ELIZABETH II | | D•G•REG•F•D•(date)
Elizabeth II, Dei Gratia Regina, Fidei Defensor
(Elizabeth II, By the Grace of God Queen and Defender of the Faith)
Portrait by: Ian Rank–Broadley

REVERSE

REVERSE 3
(used 1997 to date)
Often referred to as the 'Britannia issue' to distinguish it from the
commemorative issues.
[The seated figure of Britannia]
50 FIFTY PENCE
Design by: Christopher Ironside

Britannia - TYPE 4 (obverse 3, reverse 3)

		UNC	BU	Proof
1997	456,364,100	£0.80	£2.00	

Britannia - TYPE 5 (obverse 4, reverse 3)

		UNC	BU	Proof
1998	64,306,500	£2.00	£3.00	
1999	24,905,500	FV	£2.00	£3.00
2000	39,172,000*	FV	FV	£3.00
2001	84,999,500	FV	FV	£3.00
2002	23,757,500	FV	FV	£3.00
2003	17,551,780*	FV	FV	£3.00
2004	13,904,500*	FV	FV	£3.00
2005		FV	FV	£3.00
2006		FV	FV	£3.00
2007		FV	FV	£3.00

* (includes commemorative issues released that year)

DOCUMENTED ERRORS
1969 double-headed (minting error) £150
19?? undated "double-tailed" (minting error) £200

INFO

The "straight edges" of the 50p (and later the 20p) are not flat, but arced to form a Reuleaux polygon. Any point on an arced edge is an equal distance from the opposing vertex. This design enables the coins to be used in vending machines.

COMMEMORATIVE TYPE 1
1973 || 50 || pence (centre)
Nine clasped hands forming a circle
(Britain's entry into the European
Economic Community)
Reverse design by: David Wynne

1973			UNC	BU	Proof
1973	89,775,000		£0.80	£2.00	£3.00
	Proof in leatherette case				£3.00
	thick planchet but not recorded as Piedfort				——

COMMEMORATIVE TYPE 2
1992-1993 (upper) || 50 pence (lower)
Conference table with seats and stars
(completion of the EC single market and
the British Presidency)
Reverse design by: Mary Milner Dickens

1992-1993			UNC	BU	Proof
1992-1993	109,000	62,326	£4.00	£5.00	£9.00
	Specimen in folder (including Britannia issue)			£10.00	
	26,890	.925 sterling silver cased proof			£24.00
	15,000	.925 sterling silver Piedfort cased proof			£45.00
	1,864	.917 gold cased proof			£295.00

COMMEMORATIVE TYPE 3
50 pence (lower right)
Ships and planes taking part in the
D-Day landings
(50th Anniversary of the D-Day Invasion)
Reverse design by: John Mills

1994			UNC	BU	Proof
1994	6.705,520	66,721	£0.80	£2.00	£4.00
	Specimen in folder			£5.00	
	40,500	.925 sterling silver cased proof			£30.00
	10,000	.925 sterling silver Piedfort cased proof			£30.00
	1,877	.917 gold cased proof			£350.00

COMMEMORATIVE TYPE 4
1973 EU 1998 || 50 pence (lower)
Fireworks pattern of 12 stars
(25th Anniversary - UK entry into EEC)
Design by: John Mills

		UNC	BU	Proof
1998	5,043,000	£0.80	£2.00	£5.00
	Specimen in folder (including Britannia issue)		£10.00	
	8,854 .925 sterling silver cased proof			£20.00
	5,117 .925 sterling silver Piedfort cased proof			£40.00
	1,177 .917 gold cased proof			£225.00

COMMEMORATIVE TYPE 5
FIFTIETH ANNIVERSARY (upper) || 50 pence (lower)
Caring Hands, holding sun's rays
(50th Annirversary - National Health Service)
Design by: Mary Milner Dickens

		UNC	BU	Proof
2000	5,001,000	£0.80	£2.00	£5.00
	Specimen in folder		£5.00	
	9,029 .925 sterling silver cased proof			£20.00
	5,117 .925 sterling silver Piedfort cased proof			£40.00
	651 .917 gold cased proof			£250.00

COMMEMORATIVE TYPE 6
1850-2000 (upper) || PUBLIC LIBRARIES (lower)
Open book upon pillared building
(150th Anniversary - British Libraries)
Design by: Mary Milner Dickens

		UNC	BU	Proof
2000	Inc. with standard 2000 coin	£0.80	£2.00	£5.00
	Specimen in folder		£5.00	
	.925 sterling silver cased proof			£20.00
5,721	.925 sterling silver Piedfort cased proof			£40.00
710	.917 gold cased proof			£250.00

COMMEMORATIVE TYPE 7
50 pence (left) || 1903-2003 (lower right)
Suffragette with WSPU banner
(100th Anniversary - Women's Social and Political Union)
Design by: Mary Milner Dickens

		UNC	BU	Proof
2003	No. Inc. with standard 2003 coin	£0.80	£2.00	£5.00
	Specimen in folder		£5.00	
	.925 sterling silver cased proof			£20.00
	.925 sterling silver Piedfort cased proof			£40.00
939	.917 gold cased proof			£250.00

COMMEMORATIVE TYPE 8
50 pence (lower)
Runner's legs and stopwatch
(50th Anniversary - Roger Bannister's 4-minute mile run)
Design by: James Butler

		UNC	BU	Proof
2004	No. Inc. with standard 2004 coin	£0.80	£2.00	£5.00
	Specimen in folder		£5.00	
	.925 sterling silver cased proof			£20.00
	.925 sterling silver Piedfort cased proof			£40.00
1,250	.917 gold cased proof			£250.00

COMMEMORATIVE TYPE 9
50 (upper) || JOHNSON'S DICTIONARY 1755 (lower)
Dictionary entries for Fifty and Pence
(250th Anniversary - Samuel Johnson's English Dictionary)
Design by: Tom Phillips

		UNC	BU	Proof
2005		£0.80	£2.00	£5.00
	Specimen in folder		£5.00	
	.925 sterling silver cased proof			£20.00
5,721	.925 sterling silver Piedfort cased proof			£40.00
1,000	.917 gold cased proof			£250.00

COMMEMORATIVE TYPE 10
FIFTY PENCE (lower)
Representation of the heroic acts performed by VC recipients
(150th Anniversary - Institution of the Victoria Cross)
Design by: Clive Duncan

		UNC	BU	Proof
2006		FV	£1.00	£5.00
	Specimen in folder		£5.00	
	.925 sterling silver cased proof			£20.00
	.925 sterling silver Piedfort cased proof			£40.00
1,000	.917 gold cased proof			£250.00

COMMEMORATIVE TYPE 11
VC || FIFTY PENCE
The obverse and reverse of the Victoria Cross
(150th Anniversary - Institution of the Victoria Cross)
Design by: Claire Aldridge

		UNC	BU	Proof
2006		FV	£1.00	£5.00
	Specimen in folder		£5.00	
	.925 sterling silver cased proof			£20.00
1,000	.925 sterling silver Piedfort cased proof			£40.00
	.917 gold cased proof			£250.00

COMMEMORATIVE TYPE 12
FIFTY PENCE | 1907 | BE PREPARED | 2007
The scouting badge
(100th Anniversary - The Scout Movement)
Design by: Kerry Jones

		UNC	BU	Proof
2007		FV	£1.00	£5.00
	Specimen in folder		£6.00	
	.925 sterling silver cased proof			£28.00
1,250	.925 sterling silver Piedfort cased proof			£50.00
	.917 gold cased proof			£300.00

What's currently legal tender?

All £1 coins are legal tender. The £1 coin is the most commonly forged coin, with estimates of between 1-2% of the total £1 coins in circulation being forgeries. Look out for poor definition and mis-matching edges or reverses (i.e a Welsh reverse with a date that should have an English obverse, and/or a coin with edge lettering that doesn't match the country represented on its reverse). If someone gives you a fake £1 coin, you are not legally obliged to accept it.

Which are hard to find?

The hardest £1 coin to be found in circulation is the 1988. A relatively low mintage of just over seven million doesn't make it rare, but it's certainly the scarcest in comparison to the others.

OBVERSE

OBVERSE 1
(used 1983 - 1984)
D•G•REG•F•D•(date) || ELIZABETH II
Elizabeth II, Dei Gratia Regina, Fidei Defensor
(Elizabeth II, By the Grace of God Queen and Defender of the Faith)
Portrait by: Arnold Machin

OBVERSE 2
(used 1985 - 1997)
ELIZABETH II || D•G•REG•F•D•(date)
Elizabeth II, Dei Gratia Regina, Fidei Defensor
(Elizabeth II, By the Grace of God Queen and Defender of the Faith)
Portrait by: Raphael Maklouf

OBVERSE 3
(used 1998 to date)
ELIZABETH II•D•G || REG•F•D•(date)
Elizabeth II, Dei Gratia Regina, Fidei Defensor
(Elizabeth II, By the Grace of God Queen and Defender of the Faith)
Portrait by: Ian Rank–Broadley

UK, English and NI reverse designs carry the edge inscription:
DECUS ET TUTAMEN (An ornament and a safeguard)

Scottish reverse designs carry the edge inscription:
NEMO ME IMPUNE LACESSIT (No-one provokes me with impunity)

Welsh reverse designs carry the edge inscription:
PLEIDIOL WYF I'M GWLAD (True am I to my country)

1983 — UK Royal Arms design by: Eric Sewell

	UNC	BU	Proof
	£1.50	£2.00	£5.00
484,900 Specimen in folder		£6.00	
50,000 .925 sterling silver cased proof			£25.00
10,000 .925 sterling silver Piedfort cased proof			£115.00

The following 4 coins ("Coronet" series) were designed by Leslie Durban.

1984 — Scottish Thistle in Coronet

	UNC	BU	Proof
	£1.50	£2.00	£5.00
27,960 Specimen in folder		£6.00	
44,855 .925 sterling silver cased proof			£25.00
15,000 .925 sterling silver Piedfort cased proof			£45.00

1985 — Welsh Leek in Coronet

	UNC	BU	Proof
	£1.50	£2.00	£5.00
24,850 Specimen in folder		£6.00	
50,000 .925 sterling silver cased proof			£25.00
15,000 .925 sterling silver Piedfort cased proof			£45.00

1986 — N.I. Flax in Coronet

	UNC	BU	Proof
	£1.50	£2.00	£5.00
19,908 Specimen in folder		£6.00	
37,958 .925 sterling silver cased proof			£25.00
15,000 .925 sterling silver Piedfort cased proof			£45.00

1987 — English Oak in Coronet

	UNC	BU	Proof
	£1.50	£2.00	£5.00
72,607 Specimen in folder		£6.00	
50,500 .925 sterling silver cased proof			£25.00
15,000 .925 sterling silver Piedfort cased proof			£45.00

1988	Royal Shield design (UK) by: Derek Gorringe	UNC	BU	Proof
7,118,825		£2.00	£3.00	£5.00
29,550	Specimen in folder		£6.00	
50,000	.925 sterling silver cased proof			£25.00
10,000	.925 sterling silver Piedfort cased proof			£115.00

The following 4 coins ("Coronet" series) were designed by Leslie Durban.

1989	Scottish Thistle in Coronet	UNC	BU	Proof
70,580,501		£1.50	£2.00	£5.00
25,000	.925 sterling silver cased proof			£25.00
10,000	.925 sterling silver Piedfort cased proof			£115.00

1990	Welsh Leek in Coronet	UNC	BU	Proof
		£1.50	£2.00	£5.00
25,000	.925 sterling silver cased proof			£25.00
10,000	.925 sterling silver Piedfort cased proof			£115.00

1991	N.I. Flax in Coronet	UNC	BU	Proof
		£1.50	£2.00	£5.00
25,000	.925 sterling silver cased proof			£25.00
10,000	.925 sterling silver Piedfort cased proof			£115.00

1992	English Oak in Coronet	UNC	BU	Proof
		£1.50	£2.00	£5.00
25,000	.925 sterling silver cased proof			£25.00
10,000	.925 sterling silver Piedfort cased proof			£115.00

1993 UK Royal Arms design by: Eric Sewell

		UNC	BU	Proof
		£1.50	£2.00	£5.00
484,900	Specimen in folder		£6.00	
50,000	.925 sterling silver cased proof			£25.00
10,000	.925 sterling silver Piedfort cased proof			£115.00

The following 4 coins ("Heraldic" series) were designed by Norman Sillman.

1994 Scottish Lion Rampant

		UNC	BU	Proof
29,752,525		£1.50	£2.00	£5.00
	Specimen in folder		£6.00	
25,000	.925 sterling silver cased proof			£45.00
11,722	.925 sterling silver Piedfort cased proof			£55.00

1995 Welsh Dragon

		UNC	BU	Proof
		£1.50	£2.00	£5.00
	Specimen in folder		£6.00	
	Specimen in folder (Welsh text)		£8.00	
27,445	.925 sterling silver cased proof			£30.00
8,458	.925 sterling silver Piedfort cased proof			£50.00

1996 N.I. Celtic Cross

		UNC	BU	Proof
		£1.50	£2.00	£5.00
	Specimen in folder		£6.00	
25,000	.925 sterling silver cased proof			£35.00
10,000	.925 sterling silver Piedfort cased proof			£50.00

1997 English Three Lions

		UNC	BU	Proof
		£1.50	£2.00	£5.00
	Specimen in folder		£6.00	
20,137	.925 sterling silver cased proof			£35.00
10,000	.925 sterling silver Piedfort cased proof			£45.00

22.5 mm • 9.5 grammes • nickel-brass • lettered edge

1998   UK Royal Arms design by: Eric Sewell

		UNC	BU	Proof
(BU sets only)			£3.00	£5.00
13,843	.925 sterling silver cased proof			£30.00
10,000	.925 sterling silver Piedfort cased proof			£45.00

1999   Scottish Thistle in Coronet

		UNC	BU	Proof
(BU sets only)			£3.00	£5.00
25,000	.925 sterling silver cased proof			£30.00
2,000	.925 sterling "Special Frosted Finish" cased proof			-
10,000	.925 sterling silver Piedfort cased proof			£45.00

2000   Welsh Dragon

		UNC	BU	Proof
109,496,500		£1.50	£2.00	£5.00
40,000	.925 sterling silver cased proof			£25.00
2,000	.925 sterling "Special Frosted Finish" cased proof			-
10,000	.925 sterling silver Piedfort cased proof			£45.00

2001   N.I. Celtic Cross

		UNC	BU	Proof
58,093,731		£1.50	£2.00	£5.00
13,237	.925 sterling silver cased proof			£25.00
2,000	.925 sterling "Special Frosted Finish" cased proof			-
8,464	.925 sterling silver Piedfort cased proof			£45.00

2002   English Three Lions

		UNC	BU	Proof
77,818,000		£1.50	£2.00	£5.00
17,693	.925 sterling silver cased proof			£25.00
2,000	.925 sterling "Special Frosted Finish" cased proof			-
6,599	.925 sterling silver Piedfort cased proof			£45.00

2003	UK Royal Arms design by: Eric Sewell	UNC	BU	Proof
40,648,500		£1.50	£2.00	£5.00
13,843	.925 sterling silver cased proof			£30.00
7,894	.925 sterling silver Piedfort cased proof			£45.00

The following 4 coins ("Bridge" series) were designed by Edwina Ellis.

2004	Scotland - Forth Bridge	UNC	BU	Proof
		£1.50	£2.00	£5.00
	Specimen in folder		£6.00	
50,000	.925 sterling silver cased proof			£25.00
15,000	.925 sterling silver Piedfort cased proof			£45.00
5,000	.917 gold cased proof			£300.00

2005	Wales - Menai Bridge	UNC	BU	Proof
		£1.50	£2.00	£5.00
	Specimen in folder		£6.00	
50,000	.925 sterling silver cased proof			£25.00
15,000	.925 sterling silver Piedfort cased proof			£45.00
5,000	.917 gold cased proof			£300.00

2006	Northern Ireland - Egyptian Arch	UNC	BU	Proof
		£1.40	£2.00	£5.00
	Specimen in folder		£6.00	
50,000	.925 sterling silver cased proof			£28.00
15,000	.925 sterling silver Piedfort cased proof			£49.00
5,000	.917 gold cased proof			£325.00

2007	England - Millenium Bridge	UNC	BU	Proof
		£1.00	£2.00	£5.00
	Specimen in folder		£7.00	
20,000	.925 sterling silver cased proof			£28.00
7,500	.925 sterling silver Piedfort cased proof			£49.00
1,500	.917 gold cased proof			£440.00

43

INFO

£1 coins that have the wrong combination of date, reverse design, and edge text, are usually found to be forgeries and, as such, worthless to collectors. It is estimated that up to 2% of all £1 coins currently in circulation are counterfeits.

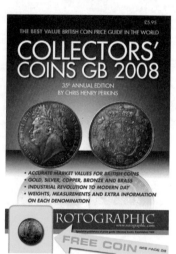

What's currently legal tender?

All £2 coins dated from 1986 to now are legal tender. The earlier single metal type coins dated 1986 to 1996 are not often seen in circulation and therefore may not be accepted by some merchants who are not familiar with them.

Which are hard to find?

All of the 1986 to 1996 (single metal) £2 coins are now hard to find in circulation. The scarcest £2 coin is probably COMMEMORATIVE TYPE 3, the 'Claim of Right' coin, as this was minted in much smaller quantities than the other 1989 £2 coin, and was only issued in Scotland. The bi-metallic coin with the 'Queen wearing a necklace' was never rare, despite the fact that some did sell for more than face value in the late 90s because people hoarded them thinking they were scarce, and this actually did cause them to be scarce, albeit temporarily!

COMMEMORATIVE TYPE 1
A thistle encircled by a laurel wreath, superimposed on St. Andrew's Cross
(1986 Commonwealth Games, Edinburgh)
Reverse design by: Norman Sillman
Edge: XIII COMMONWEALTH GAMES SCOTLAND 1986

			UNC	BU	Proof
1986	8,212,184	104,591 Proofs	£2.00	£3.00	£5.00
		Specimen in folder		£6.00	
	58,881	.500 silver UNC	£12.00		
	59,779	.925 sterling silver cased proof			£20.00

COMMEMORATIVE TYPE 2
Intertwined W & M (monogrammes of William & Mary)
House of Commons Mace, English Crown
TERCENTENARY of the BILL of RIGHTS
1689-1989
Design by: John Lobban
Edge: MILLED

			UNC	BU	Proof
1989		84,704 Proofs	£2.00	£4.00	£5.00
		Partially non frosted proof*			£6.00
		Specimen in folder		£6.00	
	25,000	.925 sterling silver cased proof			£20.00
	10,000	.925 sterling silver, Piedfort cased proof			£40.00

*Proofs that were given out in a Bass Charington promotion appear to have a non frosted bust of the Queen. More comparison is needed at this stage.

COMMEMORATIVE TYPE 3
Intertwined W & M
(monogram of William & Mary)
House of Commons Mace, Scottish Crown
TERCENTENARY of the CLAIM of RIGHT
1689-1989
Design by: John Lobban
Edge: MILLED

				UNC	BU	Proof
1989	Inc. with T2	84,704 Proofs		£5.00	£8.00	£14.00
		Specimen in folder			£14.00	
	Specimen folder, including both versions ('Bill' & 'Claim')			£22.00		
	24,852	.925 sterling silver cased proof				£25.00
	10,000	.925 sterling silver, Piedfort cased proof				£45.00

COMMEMORATIVE TYPE 4
Intertwined W & M
(monogram of William & Mary)
Britannia Seated
BANK of ENGLAND 1694-1994
Design by: Leslie Durban
Edge: SIC VOS NON VOBIS

				UNC	BU	Proof
1994	1,443,116	67,721 Proofs		£2.00	£3.00	£5.00
		Specimen in folder			£7.00	
	27,957	.925 sterling silver cased proof				£30.00
	9,569	.925 sterling silver, Piedfort cased proof				£50.00
	1,000	.917 gold cased proof				£350.00

COMMEMORATIVE TYPE 5
Dove of Peace
(Commemorating 50 years' peace,
since the end of World War II)
Reverse design by: John Mills
Edge: 1945 IN PEACE GOODWILL 1995

			UNC	BU	Proof
1995	4,388,006	60,639 Proofs	£2.00	£3.00	£4.00
		Specimen in folder		£5.00	
	50,000	.925 sterling silver cased proof			£30.00
	10,000	.925 sterling silver, Piedfort cased proof			£50.00
	2,500	.917 gold cased proof			£325.00

COMMEMORATIVE TYPE 6
UN logo, array of flags
NATIONS UNITED FOR PEACE 1945 - 1995
(50th Anniversary - United Nations)
Design by: Michael Rizzello
Edge: PLAIN MILLED

			UNC	BU	Proof
1995			£2.00	£3.00	
		Specimen in folder		£8.00	
	175,000	.925 sterling silver cased proof			£30.00
	10,000	.925 sterling silver Piedfort cased proof			£50.00
	2,098	.917 gold cased proof			£295.00

COMMEMORATIVE TYPE 7
Football design, with date, 1996, in centre
(10th European Championship)
Design by: John Mills
Edge: TENTH EUROPEAN CHAMPIONSHIP

			UNC	BU	Proof
1996	84,704		£2.00	£3.00	£4.00
		Specimen in folder		£6.00	
	50,000	.925 sterling silver cased proof			£30.00
	10,000	.925 sterling silver, Piedfort cased proof			£55.00
	2,098	.917 gold cased proof			£295.00

47

OBVERSE

OBVERSE 1
(used 1997)
ELIZABETH II DEI GRATIA REGINA F D
Elizabeth II, Dei Gratia Regina, Fidei Defensor
(Elizabeth II, By the Grace of God Queen and Defender of the Faith)
Portrait by: Raphael Maklouf

OBVERSE 2
(used 1998 to date)
ELIZABETH II DEI GRATIA REGINA FID DEF
Elizabeth II, Dei Gratia Regina, Fidei Defensor
(Elizabeth II, By the Grace of God Queen and Defender of the Faith)
Portrait by: Ian Rank–Broadley

REVERSE

REVERSE 1
(used 1997 to date)
Rings, representing stages of development:
from centre, outward: IRON AGE, INDUSTRIAL REVOLUTION
(cogs), ELECTRONIC AGE (silicon chips), INTERNET AGE
Design by: Bruce Rushin

INFO

All normal issue £2 bi-metallic
coins carry the edge inscription:
STANDING ON THE SHOULDERS OF GIANTS
Taken from a letter by Sir Isaac Newton, to a fellow
scientist, where he is quoted as saying, "If I have seen
further, it is by standing on the shoulders of giants".

TYPE 1 (obverse 1, reverse 1)

			UNC	BU	Proof
1997	13,734,625		£3.00	£4.00	£6.00
		Specimen in folder		£6.00	
	29,910	Cased silver proof			£25.00
	10,000	Cased silver piedfort proof			£50.00
	2,482	Cased gold proof			£280.00

TYPE 2 (obverse 2, reverse 1)

			UNC	BU	Proof
1998	91,110,375	100,000	FV	£3.00	£6.00
2000	25,770,000		FV	£3.00	£6.00
2001	37,843,500*		FV	FV	£6.00
2002	15,521,000*		FV	FV	£6.00
2003	15,922,250*		FV	FV	£6.00
2004			FV	FV	£6.00
2005			FV	FV	£6.00
2006			FV	FV	£6.00
2007			FV	FV	£6.00

* (includes commemorative issues released that year)

INFO

There are persistent rumours that the £2 coin with the Queen wearing a necklace are rare and worth great sums of money. These rumours are NOT true. The fact is that ALL coins dated 1997 carry the portrait of QEII designed by Raphael Maklouf, which show the Queen wearing a necklace.

TRIAL TYPE 1 (picture will be shown in the next edition)
Sailing ship, probably representing the Golden Hind
(First Bi-metallic coin trial. Coins are dated 1994 but were actually re-leased in 1998 (and are therefore not really trials at all!) The coins are all in packs which also contain examples of the outer and inner blanks and a nickel-brass ring. Obverse type is OBVERSE 1 on previous page.
Edge: DECUS ET TUTAMEN ANNO REGNI XLVI

1994	4,565		£30.00

COMMEMORATIVE TYPE 8
Symbolic representation of a stadium with rugby
ball and goalposts. '1999' above, 'TWO POUNDS' below
(1999 Rugby World Cup)
Design by: Ron Dutton
Edge: RUGBY WORLD CUP 1999

		UNC	BU	Proof
1999		£2.50	£3.00	£4.00
	Specimen in folder		£7.00	
9,665	.925 sterling silver cased proof			£30.00
10,000	.925 sterling silver Piedfort cased proof			£100.00
311	.917 gold cased proof			£250.00

COMMEMORATIVE TYPE 9
Symbolic representation of Marconi's successful
transatlantic wireless transmission of 1901,
'TWO POUNDS' below
Design by: Robert Evans
Edge: WIRELESS BRIDGES THE ATLANTIC...MARCONI 1901...

		UNC	BU	Proof
2001		£2.50	£3.00	£4.00
	Specimen in folder		£7.00	
11,488	.925 sterling silver cased proof			£25.00
6,759	.925 sterling silver Piedfort cased proof			£50.00
1,658	.917 gold cased proof			£300.00

 a
 b
 c
 d

COMMEMORATIVE TYPE 10
XVII COMMONWEALTH GAMES 2002
around athlete holding banner, (1 of 4) national flags
(27th Commonwealth Games, Manchester)
Design by: Matthew Bonaccorsi
Edge: SPIRIT OF FRIENDSHIP MANCHESTER 2002

		UNC	BU	Proof
2002	TYPE 10-a English flag	£3.00	£4.00	£6.00
	TYPE 10-b Northern Ireland flag	£3.00	£4.00	£6.00
	TYPE 10-c Scottish flag	£3.00	£4.00	£6.00
	TYPE 10-d Welsh flag	£3.00	£4.00	£6.00

Sets of the 4 coins:

	Specimens in folder	£15.00	
47,895	base metal proof set		£25.00
2,553	.925 sterling silver cased proof set		£100.00
3,497	.925 sterling silver Piedfort cased proof set		£190.00
315	.917 gold cased proof set		£1,00.00

COMMEMORATIVE TYPE 11
DNA Double Helix pattern, DNA DOUBLE HELIX,
1953 TWO POUNDS 2003
(50th Anniversary - Discovery of DNA)
Design by: John Mills
Edge: DEOXYRIBONUCLEIC ACID

		UNC	BU	Proof
2003		£2.50	£3.00	£4.00
44,090	Specimen in folder		£7.00	
9,974	.925 sterling silver cased proof			£30.00
8,632	.925 sterling silver Piedfort cased proof			£50.00
1,434	.917 gold cased proof			£295.00

28.40 mm • 12.0 grammes • bi-metal • various edge

COMMEMORATIVE TYPE 12
Steam locomotive TWO POUNDS R.TREVITHICK
1804 INVENTION INDUSTRY PROGRESS 2004
(200th Anniversary - Steam Locomotive)
Design by: Robert Lowe
Edge: pattern of arcs & curves, representing viaducts

			UNC	BU	Proof
2004			£2.50	£3.00	£4.00
		Specimen in folder		£7.00	
	25,000	.925 sterling silver cased proof			£25.00
	10,000	.925 sterling silver Piedfort cased proof			£50.00
	2,500	.917 gold cased proof			£300.00

COMMEMORATIVE TYPE 13
Swords, Maces, Croziers in a starbust pattern,
1605-2005, TWO POUNDS
(400th Anniversary - Gunpowder Plot)
Design by: Peter Forster
Edge: REMEMBER REMEMBER THE FIFTH OF NOVEMBER

			UNC	BU	Proof
2005			£2.50	£3.00	£4.00
	47,895	Specimen in folder		£7.00	
	2,553	.925 sterling silver cased proof			£30.00
	3,497	.925 sterling silver Piedfort cased proof			£50.00
	315	.917 gold cased proof			£300.00

COMMEMORATIVE TYPE 14
St. Paul's Cathedral, floodlit with spotlights.
1945-2005, TWO POUNDS
(60th Anniversary - End of World War II)
Design by: Robert Elderton
Edge: IN VICTORY: MAGNANIMITY, IN PEACE: GOODWILL*

		UNC	BU	Proof
2005		£2.50	£3.00	£4.00
	Specimen in folder		£15.00	
	Specimen folder (including special edition medallion)		£25.00	
25,000	.925 sterling silver cased proof			£25.00
Not Known	*Error edge: REMEMBER REMEMBER THE FIFTH OF NOVEMBER .925 silver cased proof, as above			£100.00+
Not Known	No edge inscription, silver cased proof			£50.00+
10,000	.925 sterling silver Piedfort cased proof			£45.00
2,500	.917 gold cased proof			£300.00

* The error edge 60th Anniversary of the End of WWII £2 coin has obviously ended up with the edge inscription of the other themed £2 coin struck that year to commemorate the gunpowder plot! The author has only been informed about one such coin and was lucky enough to have been given the opportunity to purchase it. There may be others, and the fact that the mint made this error with a proof coin may also indicate that normal 'business' struck coins might suffer from the same error. And what about the piedfort and/or gold proof versions? This is one of those discoveries that can make new coins interesting! Another example of the coin above has recently been noted in its silver proof guise with no edge inscription, just a plain milled edge. I'd be interested to hear if any other readers come across another example of the error edge or no edge inscription coins.

COMMEMORATIVE TYPE 15
Portrait of Isambard Kingdom Brunel in front of machinery
TWO POUNDS | 2006
(200th Anniversary - Birth of Isambard Kingdom Brunel)
Design by: Rod Kelly
Edge: 1806-59 . ISAMBARD KINGDOM BRUNEL . ENGINEER

		UNC	BU	Proof
2006		FV	£2.50	£4.00
	Specimen in folder		£7.00	
20,000	.925 sterling silver cased proof			£25.00
	.925 sterling silver Piedfort cased proof			£45.00
1,500	.917 gold cased proof			£330.00

28.40 mm • 12.0 grammes • bi-metal • various edge

COMMEMORATIVE TYPE 16
Representation of the engineering achievements of I.K.Brunel,
2006 | BRUNEL | TWO POUNDS
(200th Anniversary - Birth of Isambard Kingdom Brunel)
Design by: Robert Evans
Edge: SO MANY IRONS IN THE FIRE

			UNC	BU	Proof
2006			FV	£2.50	£4.00
		Specimen in folder		£7.00	
	20,000	.925 sterling silver cased proof			£30.00
	5,000	.925 sterling silver Piedfort cased proof			£50.00
	1,500	.917 gold cased proof			£330.00

COMMEMORATIVE TYPE 17
Jigsaw pieces of the English rose and Scotish thistle,
TWO | 2007 | POUNDS | 1707
(300th Anniversary - Act of Union between England and Scotland)
Design by: Yvonne Holton
Edge: UNITED INTO ONE KINGDOM

			UNC	BU	Proof
2007			FV	£2.50	£4.00
		Specimen in folder		£7.50	
	10,000	.925 sterling silver cased proof			£30.00
	5,000	.925 sterling silver Piedfort cased proof			£50.00
	750	.917 gold cased proof*			£400.00

COMMEMORATIVE TYPE 18
Five link chain with broken link as the nought in 1807,
AN ACT FOR THE ABOLITION OF THE SLAVE TRADE | 2007
(200th Anniversary - Abolition of the British slave trade)
Design by: David Gentleman
Edge: AM I NOT A MAN AND A BROTHER

			UNC	BU	Proof
2007			FV	£2.50	£4.00
		Specimen in folder		£7.50	
	10,000	.925 sterling silver cased proof			£30.00
	5,000	.925 sterling silver Piedfort cased proof			£50.00
	750	.917 gold cased proof*			£400.00

* The 2007 gold £2 coins sold out very quickly and are now no longer available new.

Britain's Only £2.50 Coin?

The coin shown below (larger than actual size), which combines elements of a 50 pence piece and elements of a £2 coin first came to light on the Predecimal.com forum a few months ago, and was purchased by the author. As errors go, they really don't come much more catastrophically mis-struck than this!

The coin is made of two parts, but unlike a normal £2 coin, both parts are cupro-nickel with no brass outer ring. The inner part is larger than it should be but bears the normal design elements from the Isambard Kingdom Brunel £2 coin (COMMEMORATIVE TYPE 15). The outer ring, which is at about a 90 degree angle to the inner part, bears all the design elements of the 2006 50p coin (COMMEMORATIVE TYPE 10), even the legend 'FIFTY PENCE' is clearly visible as is the top of the soldiers head against the top of a VC.

The coin is clearly round and has an irregularly milled edge, with no edge inscription. The inner part is the same thickness as a normal £2 coin and the outer ring is the same thickness as a normal 50p, the coin is therefore thicker in the middle and from the side has a kind of flying-saucer shape.

How this coin got to be like this is a mystery, but it was received from a bank among other normal £2 coins. Long may the Royal Mint gremlin continue to produce oddities like this, they are far more interesting that the items they make delibrately to sell to the public!

What's currently legal tender?

All £5 coins are legal tender. They are not often seen in circulation and therefore may not be accepted by some merchants who are not familiar with them. The earlier crowns should not be confused with these post-1990 £5 crowns. The crowns struck from 1972 to 1981 have a face value of 25p.

Which are hard to find?

All of these large coins are hard to find in circulation because they tend to get hoarded by the public when they are new and they are also made in lower numbers than the lower denominations. They are also heavy and not really practical to carry around for day-to-day transactions. The COMMEMORATIVE TYPE 7 with the 2000 date on the obverse seems scarcer than the 1999 dated millenium coin.

COMMEMORATIVE TYPE 1
Standard portrait of QE II
Design by: Raphael Maklouf
Double "E" monogram, crowned
Design by: Leslie Durban

			UNC	BU	Proof
1990	2,761,431		£5.00	£7.00	£10.00
	Specimen in card/folder		£10.00	£20.00	
	56,102	.925 sterling silver cased proof			£40.00
	2,750	.917 gold cased proof			£600.00

COMMEMORATIVE TYPE 2
Mary Gillick portrait of QEII
design by: Robert Elderton
St. Edward's crown
Design by: Robert Elderton

			UNC	BU	Proof
1993	1,834,655		£5.00	£7.00	£10.00
	Specimen in folder				£9.00
	75,000	.925 sterling silver cased proof			£30.00
	2,750	.917 gold cased proof			£630.00

56

COMMEMORATIVE TYPE 3
Standard portrait of QE II
Design by: Raphael Maklouf
Windsor Castle and Pennants
Design by: Avril Vaughan
Edge:
VIVAT REGINA ELIZABETHA

			UNC	BU	Proof
1996	2,396,100		£5.00	£7.00	£10.00
		Specimen in folder		£9.00	
	75,000	.925 sterling silver cased proof			£30.00
	2,750	.917 gold cased proof			£630.00

COMMEMORATIVE TYPE 4
Conjoined busts of Elizabeth II
and Prince Philip
Design by: Philip Nathan
Arms of the Royal Couple,
crown, anchor. *Design by: Leslie Durban*

			UNC	BU	Proof
1997	1,733,000		£5.00	£7.00	£10.00
		Specimen in folder		£9.00	
	33,689	.925 sterling silver cased proof			£30.00
	2,750	.917 gold cased proof			£630.00

COMMEMORATIVE TYPE 5
Standard portrait of QE II
Design by: Ian Rank–Broadley
Prince Charles, "The Prince's Trust"
Design by: Michael Noakes

				UNC	BU	Proof
1998	1,407,300	100,000		£5.00	£7.00	£10.00
		Specimen in folder			£9.00	
	35,000	.925 sterling silver cased proof				£30.00
	2,000	.917 gold cased proof				£630.00

38.61 mm • 28.28 grammes • cupro-nickel • various edge

COMMEMORATIVE TYPE 6
Standard portrait of QEII
Design by: Ian Rank-Broadley
Portrait of Princess Diana
Design by: David Cornell

		UNC	BU	Proof
1999		£5.00	£7.00	£10.00
	Specimen in folder		£9.00	
49,545	.925 sterling silver cased proof			£30.00
2,750	.917 gold cased proof			£630.00

COMMEMORATIVE TYPE 7
Standard portrait of QE II
(Dated either 1999 or 2000)
Design by: Ian Rank-Broadley
Clock at midnight, with map of British Isles
Design by: Jeffrey Matthews
edge: WHAT'S PAST IS PROLOGUE

		UNC	BU	Proof
Dated 1999 on Obverse		£5.00	£7.00	£10.00
	Specimen in folder		£11.00	
75,000	.925 sterling silver cased proof			£40.00
2,750	.917 gold cased proof			£600.00
Dated 2000 on Obverse (not shown)		£7.00	£9.00	£14.00
	Specimen in folder		£15.00	
75,000	.925 sterling silver cased proof			£40.00
2,750	.917 gold cased proof			£600.00

COMMEMORATIVE TYPE 7a

Special mintmarked piece, available only at the Millennium Dome.

2000	Specimen in folder	£25.00

COMMEMORATIVE TYPE 8
Standard portrait of QE II
Design by: Ian Rank–Broadley
Portrait of the Queen Mother
Design by: Ian Rank–Broadley

		UNC	BU	Proof
2000		£5.00	£7.00	£10.00
	Specimen in folder		£11.00	
100,000	.925 sterling silver cased proof			£35.00
14,850	.925 sterling silver Piedfort cased proof			£65.00
2,750	.917 gold cased proof			£625.00

COMMEMORATIVE TYPE 9
Standard portrait of QEII
Design by: Ian Rank–Broadley
Wyon portrait of Victoria
Design by: Mary Milner Dickens

			UNC	BU	Proof
2001	851,491		£5.00	£7.00	£10.00
	44,090	Specimen in folder		£11.00	
	19,812	.925 sterling silver cased proof			£35.00
	2,831	.917 gold cased proof			£600.00

38.61 mm • 28.28 grammes • cupro-nickel • various edge

COMMEMORATIVE TYPE 10
Queen Elizabeth II on horseback
Design by: Ian Rank–Broadley
Queen wearing robes and diadem
Design by: Ian Rank–Broadley

			UNC	BU	Proof
2002			£5.00	£7.00	£10.00
	340,230	Specimen in folder		£11.00	
	54,012	.925 sterling silver cased proof			£35.00
	3,461	.917 gold cased proof			£600.00

COMMEMORATIVE TYPE 11
Standard portrait of QEII
Design by: Ian Rank–Broadley
Portrait of Queen Mother
Design by: Avril Vaughan. edge:
**STRENGTH DIGNITY
LAUGHTER**

			UNC	BU	Proof
2002			£5.00	£7.00	£10.00
		Specimen in folder		£11.00	
	35,000	.925 sterling silver cased proof			£35.00
	2,750	.917 gold cased proof			£600.00

COMMEMORATIVE TYPE 12
Sketched portrait of QE II
Design by: Tom Philips
"GOD SAVE THE QUEEN"
Design by: Tom Philips

			UNC	BU	Proof
2003	1,307,010		£5.00	£7.00	£10.00
		Specimen in folder		£9.00	
	75,000	.925 sterling silver cased proof			£30.00
	3,500	.917 gold cased proof			£620.00

COMMEMORATIVE TYPE 13
Standard portrait of QEII
Design by: Ian Rank–Broadley
Conjoined Britannia and
Marianne
Design by: David Gentlemen

		UNC	BU	Proof
2004		£5.00	£7.00	£10.00
15,000	.925 sterling silver cased proof			£30.00
1,500	.917 gold cased proof			£620.00
501	.9995 platinum cased proof (3.0271 troy oz)			-

COMMEMORATIVE TYPE 14
Standard portrait of QE II
design by: Ian Rank–Broadley
Portrait of Horatio Nelson
design by: James Butler

		UNC	BU	Proof
2005		£5.00	£7.00	£10.00
	Specimen in folder		£11.00	
75,000	.925 sterling silver cased proof			£30.00
2,500	.917 gold cased proof			£600.00

COMMEMORATIVE TYPE 15
Standard portrait of QEII
design by: Ian Rank–Broadley
HMS Victory & Temeraire
design by: Clive Duncan

		UNC	BU	Proof
2005		£5.00	£7.00	£10.00
	Specimen in folder			£11.00
	Specimen set (contains both 2005 folders, in sleeve)		£25.00	
75,000	.925 sterling silver cased proof			£30.00
2,750	.917 gold cased proof			£620.00

COMMEMORATIVE TYPE 16
Standard portrait of QEII
Design by: Ian Rank–Broadley
Ceremonial Trumpets
with Banners
Design by: Danuta Solowiej–Wedderburn

			UNC	BU	Proof
2006			£5.00	£7.00	£10.00
		Specimen in folder		£9.00	
	75,000	.925 sterling silver			£30.00
	2,750	.917 gold			£620.00

COMMEMORATIVE TYPE 17
Standard portrait of QEII
Design by: Ian Rank–Broadley
The North Rose Window at
Westminster Abbey
Design by: Emma Noble

			UNC	BU	Proof
2007			£5.00	£7.00	£10.00
		Specimen in folder		£10.00	
	35,000	.925 sterling silver			£40.00
	5,000	.925 sterling silver piedfort proof			£80.00
	2,500	.917 gold			£925.00

United Kingdom banknotes

The UK currently has four denominations of legal tender banknotes in circulation; the £5, £10, £20 and £50 notes. Some banks in Scotland and in Northern Ireland also issue Sterling banknotes in the same denomination as the Bank of England types. These notes are not officially legal tender but they are of course readily accepted within the provinces in which they circulate. All of the Scottish and Northern Irish banknotes have to be backed up by Bank of England money; in other words, a bank issuing notes in Scotland or Northern Ireland has to hold in its vaults the same amount of Bank of England money. Usually this Bank of England money is held in the form of special high-value banknotes that are exchanged just between banks. The circulating Scottish and Northern Ireland banknotes are not covered in this book (but will hopefully be included in a future edition).

The four currently circulating Bank of England notes are:

£5 - Mainly green with Elizabeth Fry on the reverse.
£10 - Mainly orange with Charles Darwin on the reverse.
£20 - Mainly purple with Edward Elgar or Adam Smith on the reverse.
£50 - Mainly red with Sir John Houblon on the reverse.

The 'promise to pay the bearer' on each Bank of England banknote never expires, even when the notes of that type have long since been removed from circulation. As a result, every single Bank of England note can always be redeemed for its face value at the Bank of England, or any UK bank (including old Bank of England £1 and 10 Shilling notes). Shopkeepers and other merchants are not obliged to accept older Bank of England notes. Before redeeming older Bank of England notes it's obviously a good idea to check that they don't have a collectable worth first. This can be done using the Rotographic publication "Collectors' Banknotes" which is published regularly and includes valuations for all Bank of England and HM Treasury issued banknotes.

Banknote condition

Just as with coins, condition plays a very important role when the values of banknotes are concerned. Most collectors will attempt to collect the banknotes in the best condition they can afford. With modern banknotes this will nearly always be uncirculated (mint condition) examples, as such examples of modern banknotes are usually obtainable. With this in mind, most well-used, tatty, creased and dirty banknotes that have exchanged hands many times are only likely to be worth their face value. EF is an abbreviation for Extremely Fine and means that a note is in very good condition, but just a little way from being classed as UNCirculated. VF means Very Fine and is quite a common grade for modern notes that have seen limited average use.

Serial numbers

Collectors like interesting serial numbers too. If you ever get given a note with a low serial number, where at least the first 3 digits of the 6 digit number are zeros, keep hold of it. A note with the serial number AH43 000954 will be slightly more interesting than AH43 874563, for example. The note AH43 000001 would of course be more interesting still. AA01 000045 would be even more desirable! Collectors also like interesting patterns in numbers, like AH43 434343, AH22 222222 or AH12 345678. You won't get offered huge amounts of money for notes with interesting serial numbers, but you might persuade someone to give you slightly more than face value, assuming the note is in good condition.

Signed by <u>Merlyn Lowther</u>, the chief cashier of the Bank of England from 1999 to 2003.

DETAILS	EF	UNC

Letter, Letter, Number, Number, followed by 6 digits

	EF	UNC
Number AA01 000000 Special Specimen note		£800.00
Prefix HA01 followed by 6 digits (special first run)	£6.00	£15.00
Prefix HC01 followed by 6 digits (first prefix)	£40.00	£75.00
Prefix JA** followed by 6 digits (last prefix of first type)	£7.00	£15.00
Prefix JA90 followed by 6 digits (with missing varnish on serial number)	£9.00	£30.00
Prefix DL25 followed by 6 digits (special column sort prefix)	£7.00	£20.00
Prefix X*** followed by 6 digits (varnish trial prefix)	£20.00	£90.00
Prefix LL** followed by 6 digits (replacement notes)	£7.00	£20.00
Prefix ER50 followed by 6 digits (special presentation pack issue)*		-
Prefix HM02 followed by 6 digits (special presentation pack issue)*		-
Prefix HM03 followed by 6 digits (special presentation pack issue)*		-
Prefix QC03 followed by 6 digits (special presentation pack issue)*		-
Prefix QC50 followed by 6 digits (special presentation pack issue)*		-
Prefix YR20 followed by 6 digits (special presentation pack issue)*		-
Prefix QM20 followed by 6 digits (special presentation pack issue)*		-
Prefix QV20 followed by 6 digits (special presentation pack issue)*		-
Prefix GJ20 followed by 6 digits (special presentation pack issue)*		-

* These notes were only issued as part of special sets; it is therefore hard to value them on their own. None of these notes should have been circulated, so if you find one, it should certainly be worth more than its face value.

Signed by <u>Andrew Bailey</u>, the chief cashier of the Bank of England from 2004 to date.

DETAILS	UNC

Letter, Letter, Number, Number, followed by 6 digits

	EF	UNC
Prefix JB46 followed by 6 digits (first prefix)	£25.00	£60.00
Prefix EL** followed by 6 digits (special column sort prefix)	£6.00	£12.00

Signed by <u>Merlyn Lowther</u>, the chief cashier of the Bank of England from 1999 to 2003.

DETAILS	VF	EF	UNC
Letter, Letter, Number, Number, followed by 6 digits			
Number AA01 000000 Special Specimen note			£800.00
Prefix AA01 followed by 6 digits (first prefix)		£14.00	£30.00
Prefix AA01 followed by 6 digits (first prefix, worded 'and company')*¹		£30.00	£50.00
Prefix AD** followed by 6 digits (worded 'and company')*¹		£40.00	£80.00
Prefix AH80 followed by 6 digits (last prefix of first type) £25.00		£100.00	£200.00
Prefix AJ** followed by 6 digits (first production run)		£12.00	£20.00
Prefix EL** followed by 6 digits (special column sort prefix)		£15.00	£30.00
Prefix LL** followed by 6 digits (replacement notes)		£30.00	£70.00
Prefix LL** followed by 6 digits (replacement notes 'and company')*		£12.00	£30.00
Prefix CC77 followed by 6 digits (highest prefix known*²) £20.00		£40.00	£80.00
Prefix M*** followed by 6 digits (experimental notes) £80.00		£200.00	
Prefix ER50 followed by 6 digits (special presentation pack issue)*			-
Prefix QC50 followed by 6 digits (special presentation pack issue)*			-
Prefix QV10 followed by 6 digits (special presentation pack issue)*			-
Prefix VR10 followed by 6 digits (special presentation pack issue)*			-

* These notes were only issued as part of special sets; it is therefore hard to value them on their own. None of these notes should have been circulated, so if you find one, it should certainly be worth more than its face value.

*¹ These notes have the correct wording 'The Governor and Company of the Bank of England' in the band of text above the central oval where the Queen's watermark appears. A variety exists with the wording 'The Governor <u>and the</u> Company of the Bank of England'. Both types were made in high numbers.

*2 The CC** prefix overlaps with the CC** Bailey notes below. Until recently it was thought that CC40 was the last Lowther prefix. This is not that case as at the time of writing (in 2008) CC77 prefixes have been noted on newly issued Lowther notes. Higher CC prefixes may exist and the highest or last known will always attract a premium.

Signed by <u>Andrew Bailey</u>, the chief cashier of the Bank of England from 2004 to date.

DETAILS	EF	UNC
Letter, Letter, Number, Number, followed by 6 digits		
Prefix CC41 followed by 6 digits (lowest known prefix)	£50.00	£150.00
Prefix EL** followed by 6 digits (special column sort prefix)	£12.00	£20.00
Prefix HL** followed by 6 digits (special column sort prefix)	£18.00	£30.00
Prefix LL** followed by 6 digits (replacement notes)	£14.00	£25.00

Signed by <u>Merlyn Lowther</u>, the chief cashier of the Bank of England from 1999 to 2003.

DETAILS	EF	UNC

Letter, Letter, Number, Number, followed by 6 digits (Elgar Reverse)

	EF	UNC
Number AA01 000000 Special Specimen note		£800.00
Prefix AA01 followed by 6 digits (first prefix)	£25.00	£45.00
Prefix AL** followed by 6 digits (special column sort prefix)	£25.00	£35.00
Prefix DE80 followed by 6 digits (last prefix)	£75.00	£150.00
Prefix LL01 followed by 6 digits (first prefix of replacement notes)	£60.00	£140.00
Prefix LL** (replacement notes)	£30.00	£60.00
Prefixes ER50, QC50, QM10, VR10, YR20 (special presentation pack issue)*		-

* These notes were only issued as part of special sets; it is therefore hard to value them on their own. None of these notes should have been circulated, so if you find one, it should certainly be worth more than its face value.

Signed by <u>Andrew Bailey</u>, the chief cashier of the Bank of England from 2004 to date.

DETAILS	EF	UNC
Letter, Letter, Number, Number, followed by 6 digits (Elgar Reverse)		
Prefix DE41 followed by 6 digits (first prefix)	£70.00	£120.00
Prefix BL** followed by 6 digits (special column sort prefix)	£25.00	£35.00
Prefix LL** followed by 6 digits (replacement notes)	£40.00	£25.00
Letter, Letter, Number, Number, followed by 6 digits (New Smith Reverse)		
Too little is known about the prefixes used at the time of writing		-

Signed by <u>G E A Kentfield</u>, the chief cashier of the Bank of England from 1991 to 1998.

The £50 is the only Kentfield note left in circulation. This is because the design has not been changed since these were issued in 1994. The other notes have all been updated and during that process the older (Kentfield) types were removed from circulation.

DETAILS	EF	UNC
Letter, Number, Number, followed by 6 digits		
Prefix A01 followed by 6 digits (first prefix)	£80.00	£150.00
Prefix H98 followed by 6 digits (last prefix)	£150.00	£220.00
Prefix H99 followed by 6 digits (special print run for sets)	£75.00	£120.00
Prefix L** followed by 6 digits (special column sort prefix)	£75.00	£130.00
Prefix A99 folowed by 6 digits (experimental prefix)	£80.00	£140.00
Prefix M99 followed by 6 digits (experimental prefix)	£150.00	£300.00
Letter, Letter, Number, Number, followed by 6 digits		
LL** followed by 6 digits (replacement note prefix)	£90.00	£200.00

Signed by <u>Merlyn Lowther</u>, the chief cashier of the Bank of England from 1999 to 2003.

DETAILS	EF	UNC
Letter, Number, Number, followed by 6 digits		
Number J01 followed by 6 digits (first prefix)	£80.00	£150.00
Prefix L** followed by 6 digits (special column sort prefix)	£60.00	£100.00
Prefix M35 followed by 6 digits (last prefix)	£80.00	£180.00
Prefix M01 followed by 6 digits (first prefix of last run)	£80.00	£150.00

Signed by <u>Andrew Bailey</u>, the chief cashier of the Bank of England from 2004 to date.

DETAILS	EF	UNC
Letter, Number, Number, followed by 6 digits		
Prefix M01 followed by 6 digits (first prefix)	£70.00	£150.00

From 1971 to 1982, The Royal Mint issued proof coin sets sealed in plastic, enclosed in lightweight card envelopes.

Year	Pieces	Coins	Notes
1971	6	½p, 1p, 2p, 5p, 10p, 50p	
1972	7	½p, 1p, 2p, 5p, 10p, 25p, 50p	Silver Wedding crown
1973	6	½p, 1p, 2p, 5p, 10p, 50p	
1974	6	½p, 1p, 2p, 5p, 10p, 50p	
1975	6	½p, 1p, 2p, 5p, 10p, 50p	
1976	6	½p, 1p, 2p, 5p, 10p, 50p	
1977	7	½p, 1p, 2p, 5p, 10p, 25p, 50p	Silver Jubilee crown
1978	6	½p, 1p, 2p, 5p, 10p, 50p	
1979	6	½p, 1p, 2p, 5p, 10p, 50p	
1980	6	½p, 1p, 2p, 5p, 10p, 50p	
1981	6	½p, 1p, 2p, 5p, 10p, 50p	
1982	7	½p, 1p, 2p, 5p, 10p, 20p, 50p	new 20p added

In 1983, the packaging was changed to a blue leatherette bookshelf type case.

Year	Pieces	Coins	Notes
1983	8	½p, 1p, 2p, 5p, 10p, 20p, 50p, £1	new £1 added
1984	8	½p, 1p, 2p, 5p, 10p, 20p, 50p, £1	

INFO

The current secondary market for Proof sets is very volatile and unpredictable. As a rule of thumb, it would be conservative to set the value of these sets at approximately 4 to 5 times the face value of the coins included, for standard sets. For deluxe sets, add 20% more to that figure. Some sets, especially the most recent releases, contain commemoratives that might become "hot" on the market, which would also greatly influence the market price for the set. Until the secondary market becomes better established, and more reputable dealers begin carrying these sets regularly, it is too difficult to attempt to determine what values the market will sustain on these sets. Collectors always prefer sets in mint condition with no toning affecting the coins.

Beginning in 1985, two types of packaging were offered: The "standard" blue leatherette case, and the "deluxe" red leather case.

Year	Pieces	Coins	Notes
1985	7	1p, 2p, 5p, 10p, 20p, 50p, £1	½p removed
1986	8	1p, 2p, 5p, 10p, 20p, 50p, £1, £2	Commonwealth Games
1987	7	1p, 2p, 5p, 10p, 20p, 50p, £1	
1988	7	1p, 2p, 5p, 10p, 20p, 50p, £1	
1989	9	1p, 2p, 5p, 10p, 20p, 50p, £1, £2, £2	Bill of Rights / Claim of Right
1990	8	1p, 2p, 5p, 5p, 10p, 20p, 50p, £1	Both 5p sizes
1991	7	1p, 2p, 5p, 10p, 20p, 50p, £1	
1992	9	1p, 2p, 5p, 10p, 10p, 20p, 50p, 50p, £1	Both 10p sizes; EEC 50p
1993	8	1p, 2p, 5p, 10p, 20p, 50p, £1, £5	Coronation Anniversary
1994	8	1p, 2p, 5p, 10p, 20p, 50p, £1, £2	Bank of England
1995	8	1p, 2p, 5p, 10p, 20p, 50p, £1, £2	Dove of Peace
1996	9	1p, 2p, 5p, 10p, 20p, 50p, £1, £2, £5	Football; 70th Birthday
1997	10	1p, 2p, 5p, 10p, 20p, 50p, 50p, £1, £2, £5	Both 50p's; Royal Wedding
1998	10	1p, 2p, 5p, 10p, 20p, 50p, 50p, £1, £2, £5	EU; Prince Charles
1999	9	1p, 2p, 5p, 10p, 20p, 50p, £1, £2, £5	Rugby, Princess Diana

Beginning with the listings for 2000, it is accepted that all sets will contain the standard 8 pieces: 1p, 2p, 5p, 10p, 20p, 50p (Britannia issue), £1, and £2 (bi-metallic "4 Ages of Man"). The Royal Mint, also produce deluxe proof sets and executive proof sets, which contain the same coins but have better packaging. The deluxe sets are sold for a few pounds more than the standard sets and the executive sets are sold for about twice the price of the standard sets.

Year	Pieces	Commemorative issues
2000	10	50p Public Libraries, £5 Millennium
2001	10	£2 Marconi, £5 Victorian Era
2002	9	£5 Coronation Jubilee
2003	11	50p Women's Suffrage, £2 DNA, £5 Golden Jubilee
2004	10	50p Roger Bannister, £2 Trevithick's Steam Locomotive
2005	12	50p Johnson's Dictionary, £2 Guy Fawkes, £5 Nelson, £5 Trafalgar
2006	13	Both VC 50p's, Both Brunel £2's, £5 Queen's 80th Birthday
2007	12	50p Scouting, Union £2 and Slave Trade £2, Diamond Wedding £5

In 1982, the Royal Mint introduced BU sets, which contain most of the coins contained in the Proof sets (crowns normally not included). These sets do not have the proof quality striking, and are packaged in a folder style, but they do provide history background text on the coins.

Year	Pieces	Coins	Notes
1982	7	½p, 1p, 2p, 5p, 10p, 20p, 50p	
1983	8	½p, 1p, 2p, 5p, 10p, 20p, 50p, £1	new £1 added
1984	8	½p, 1p, 2p, 5p, 10p, 20p, 50p, £1	
1985	7	1p, 2p, 5p, 10p, 20p, 50p, £1	½p removed
1986	8	1p, 2p, 5p, 10p, 20p, 50p, £1, £2	Commonwealth Games
1987	7	1p, 2p, 5p, 10p, 20p, 50p, £1	
1988	7	1p, 2p, 5p, 10p, 20p, 50p, £1	
1989	7	1p, 2p, 5p, 10p, 20p, 50p, £1	
1990	8	1p, 2p, 5p, 5p, 10p, 20p, 50p, £1	lg & sm 5p
1991	7	1p, 2p, 5p, 10p, 20p, 50p, £1	
1992	9	1p, 2p, 5p, 10p, 10p, 20p, 50p, 50p, £1	lg & sm 10p; EEC
1993	8	1p, 2p, 5p, 10p, 20p, 50p, £1, £5	Coronation Anniversary
1994	8	1p, 2p, 5p, 10p, 20p, 50p, £1, £2	Bank of England
1995	8	1p, 2p, 5p, 10p, 20p, 50p, £1, £2	Dove of Peace
1996	8	1p, 2p, 5p, 10p, 20p, 50p, £1, £2	Football
1997	9	1p, 2p, 5p, 10p, 20p, 50p, 50p, £1, £2	lg & sm 50p
1998	9	1p, 2p, 5p, 10p, 20p, 50p, 50p, £1, £2	EU
1999	8	1p, 2p, 5p, 10p, 20p, 50p, £1, £2	Rugby
2000	9	1p, 2p, 5p, 10p, 20p, 50p, 50p, £1, £2	Public Libraries
2001	9	1p, 2p, 5p, 10p, 20p, 50p, £1, £2, £2	Marconi
2002	8	1p, 2p, 5p, 10p, 20p, 50p, £1, £2	
2003	10	1p, 2p, 5p, 10p, 20p, 50p, 50p, £1, £2, £2	Women's Suffrage, DNA
2004	10	1p, 2p, 5p, 10p, 20p, 50p, 50p, £1, £2, £2	Bannister, Trevithick
2005	10	1p, 2p, 5p, 10p, 20p, 50p, 50p, £1, £2, £2	Dictionary, Guy Fawkes
2006	10	1p, 2p, 5p, 10p, 20p, 50p, 50p, £1, £2, £2	Victoria Cross, Brunel
2007	9	1p, 2p, 5p, 10p, 20p., 50p, £1, £2, £2	Slave trade, Act of Union

The above sets tend to sell from between 2x to 3x the face value of the coins included. Sets in mint condition with absolutely no toning on any of the coins will attract a premium.

Year	Pieces	Coins
1983	7	½p, 1p, 2p, 5p, 10p, 20p, 50p Specially packaged set for the H J Heinz Company.
1983	8	½p, 1p, 2p, 5p, 10p, 20p, 50p, £1 Specially packaged set for the Martini & Rossi Company.
1988	7	1p, 2p, 5p, 10p, 20p, 50p, £1 Special package celebrating Australia's Bicentennial.
1996	14 (7+7)	1p, 2p, 5p, 10p, 20p, 50p, £1; pre-decimal 1/2d, 1d, 3d, 6d, 1/, 2/, 2/6d Special package commemorating 25 years of decimalisation.
2000	9	1p,2p,5p,10p,20p,50p,£1,£2, £5 (Millennium) In special "Time Capsule" packaging.
2004	3	50p (Roger Bannister), £1 (Forth bridge), £2 (Trevithick's Locomotive) "Celebrating Human Achievement"
2005	3	50p (Johnson's dictionary), £1 (Menai bridge), £2 (Guy Fawkes) new packaging of commemorative issues

The sets above were specially marketed for commemorative or promotional purposes.

INFO

1998 saw the introduction of yet another Royal Mint packaging, the "Baby Pack". These sets contain the same coins as the normal BU sets, but the packaging is oriented as gifts for newborn children, with a card to provide information about the child's family tree, etc. Continuing on this course, in 1999, the "Wedding Pack" was introduced.

The following are sterling (.925) silver proof sets, designed for various occasions, including the introduction of the coins themselves. These are normally found in hard acrylic capsules, enclosed in a clam-shell case, and with a certificate from the Royal Mint. Loose pieces, without the case and / or certificate, sell at a deep discount, up to 40% less.

Five Pence

1990	35,000	large & small sized pair	£25.00

Ten Pence

1992	35,000	large & small sized pair	£25.00

Fifty Pence

1997	10,304	large & small sized pair	£25.00
1998	22,078	NHS issue and EU issue pair	£55.00
1998		pair, EU silver proof & EU silver Piedfort	£70.00

One Pound

1983 - 88	1,000	set of 6 regional designs, Arms, Shield	£75.00
1984 - 87	50,000	set of 4 regional designs	£90.00
1994 - 97	25,000	set of 4 regional designs	£100.00
1999 - 2002	25,000	set of 4 regional designs	£100.00

Two Pounds

1989	25,000	Bill of Rights & Claim of Rights pair	£60.00
1997	40,000	new bi-metallic circulation issue	£20.00
1998	25,000	new portrait on the circulation issue	£20.00
1997/98		bi-metallic Maklouf & Rank-Broadley pair	£35.00

INFO

We are reluctant to list prices for these at this time, as we are still monitoring activity, in order to determine the fair value that the market can sustain. One day, information is received about a set selling for £30, while days later, a similar set sells for £4. As more information is gathered, and more dealers begin establishing basic buy/ sell pricing, a true "fair market value" can be determined.

Year	Qty	Description	Price
1981	5,000	set, all issues, 1/2p-50p in base metals, sterling 25p commemorative, 22k gold Sovereign & £5	£700.00
1981		pair, sterling 25p commemorative, 22k gold Sovereign	£70.00
1992	1,000	set, both lg and sm 10p, 50p EEC, and £1	£75.00
1993	1,000	set, 50p EEC, £1, and £5 Coronation commem.	£75.00
1994	2,000	set, 50p D-Day, £1, and £2 Bank of England	£70.00
1995	1,000	silver set, peace £2, UN £2 and £1 coin	£50.00
1996	1,000	silver set, £5, £2 and £1 coins	£50.00
1996		set, all issues, 1p-£1 (25th Anniversary of Decimalisation)	£70.00
	500	pair, 1996 70th Birthday crown & 1997 Royal Wedding Jubilee crown	£60.00
1997		set, 50p, £1, £2, £5 Wedding Jubilee, £2 Britannia	£120.00
1999		set, £5 Millennium, £2 Britannia	£40.00
1999		set, £2 Britannia, £10 stamp	
2000	13,180	set, 1p-£5 Millennium, plus Maundy set (13 pieces)	£200.00
2000		£5 Millennium, plus YR2000 serial numbered £20 note	
		pair, 2002 Silver Jubilee crown & 2003 Coronation Jubilee crown	£60.00
2004		pair, 2004 Entente Cordiale crown & French €1 1/2 commem.	£75.00
2004	750	set, 50p Bannister, £1 Forth Bridge, £2 Trevithick, £5 Entente Cordiale £2 Britannia.	£75.00
asst'd		1999, 2001, 2002, 2003 £2 Britannia uncirculated.	£45.00

The following set was struck in .917 (22K) gold.

Year	Qty	Description	Price
2002	2,002	set, 1p-£5 Golden Jubilee, plus Maundy set (13 pieces)	£750.00

ALERT

It seems that official Royal Mint cases are obtainable, and some of these sets are assembled on the secondary market, with the individual coins and accompanying certificates. Original RM-issued sets usually contain a single certificate, listing each coin in the set.

77

Piedforts are pieces that are double the thickness and weight of normal pieces, and are almost always struck in sterling (.925) silver. These are normally found in hard acrylic capsules, enclosed in a clam-shell case, and with a certificate from the Royal Mint. Loose pieces, without the case and/or certificate sell at a deep discount, up to 40% less.

Five Pence
1990	20,000	.925 sterling silver, small size Piedfort	£20.00

Ten Pence
1992		.925 sterling silver, small size Piedfort	£30.00

Twenty Pence
1982		.925 sterling silver, Piedfort	£30.00

Fifty Pence
1997	7,192	.925 sterling silver, small size Piedfort	£50.00
1998		EEC & NHS pair, Piedfort	£30.00

One Pound
1983 - 88	500	set of 6 regional designs, Arms, Shield, Piedfort	£250.00
1984 - 87	10,000	.925 sterling silver, proof set of 4 Piedfort	£175.00
1994 - 97		.925 sterling silver, proof set of 4 Piedfort	£190.00
1999-2002	10,000	.925 sterling silver, proof set of 4 Piedfort	£225.00
2004-2007	1,400	.925 sterling silver, proof set of 4 Piedfort	£200.00

Two Pounds
1989	10,000	Bill of Rights & Claim of Rights pair, Piedfort	£30.00
1997	10,000	.925 sterling silver, Piedfort	£55.00
1998	10,000	.925 sterling silver, Piedfort £55	
1997/98	.10,000	925 sterling silver, Piedfort (pair)	£125.00
1999	10,000	.925 sterling silver, proof Piedfort HOLOGRAM	£100.00

Five Pounds
2005		Nelson & Trafalgar pair, Piedfort	£125.00

Sets
2003		set, 50p WPSU, £1 Royal Arms, £2 DNA Piedfort	£60.00
2004	7500	set, 50p Bannister, £1 Forth Bridge, £2 Trevithick Piedfort	£150.00
2005		set, 50p Johnson's Dictionary, £1 Menai Bridge, £2 GunPowder Plot, £2 World War II Piedfort	£150.00
2007		£5, both £2 coins, £1 and 50p Piedfort	£250.00

Special Collector Issues (Patterns)

2005   A trial bi-metallic piece was issued in 1994 (predecessor to the £2 bi-metallic). The obverse shows a cutty (ship), while the reverse carries the Maklouf portrait of QEII. The ring bears the legend "ROYAL MINT TRIAL PATTERN", and an edge legend of 'ANNO REGNIA XLVI, DECUS ET TUTAMEN"

Pattern sets issued by the Royal Mint to preview the new issue of "Bridges" £1 coins. All of these coins carry the date of 2003, and rather than having a face value, they are labelled as "PATTERN".

| 2003 | 7,500 | .925 sterling silver, 7,500 , proof set of 4 | £100.00 |
| | 3,000 | .917 gold proof set of 4 | £1,200.00 |

A continuation of the above set, this set shows the "Beasts" series, which was a runner-up in the design competition for the new £1 coinage. All of these coins carry the date of 2004, and rather than having a face value, they are labelled as "PATTERN". Issued, as listed, in both sterling (.925) silver, and 22k (.917) gold.

| 2004 | 5,000 | .925 sterling silver, proof set of 4 | £95.00 |
| | 2,250 | .917 gold proof set of 4 | £975.00 |

Silver Britannia issues began in 1997, with proof-only issues. Commencing in 1998, the RM has created a pattern of using the standard Standing Britannia for every other year (even years), while bringing out new unique designs for the odd years. All reverse designs to date are from Philip Nathan.

Bullion .958 Silver (UNC) £2 issues

1998	88,909	Standing Britannia	£15.00
1999	69,394	Britannia in Chariot	£15.00
2000	81,301	Standing Britannia	£15.00
2001	44,816	Una & the Lion	£15.00
2002	48,215	Standing Britannia	£15.00
2003	73,271	Helmeted Britannia facing left	£18.00
2004	100,000	Standing Britannia	£18.00
2005	100,000	Britannia seated	£18.00
2006		Standing Britannia	£18.00
2007		Britannia seated	£16.00

Collectors .958 Silver (PROOF) issues

1997	£2	4,173	Britannia in Chariot	£50.00
	20p	8,686		£15.00
1998	£2	2,168	Standing Britannia	£90.00
	20p	2,724		£15.00
2001	£2	3,047	Britannia with Lion	£50.00
	20p	826		£20.00
2003	£2	1,833	Britannia wearing Roman Helmet	£50.00
	20p	1,003		£15.00
2004	£2	5,000	Standing Britannia	£50.00
2005	£2	2,500	Britannia seated	£50.00
2006	£2	2,500	Standing Britannia	£50.00
2007	£2		Britannia seated	£50.00
2007	20p		Britannia seated	£20.00

Special Collectors' (PROOF) sets

1997	11,832	Set of 4 (£2, £1, 50p, 20p)	£125.00
1998	3,044	Set of 4 (£2, £1, 50p, 20p)	£170.00
2001	4,596	Set of 4 (£2, £1, 50p, 20p)	£95.00
2003	3,623	Set of 4 (£2, £1, 50p, 20p)	£90.00
2005	5,000	Set of 4 (£2, £1, 50p, 20p)	£90.00
2006	-	Set of 5x different £2 with gold plated details	£210.00
2007	2,500	Set of 4 (£2, £1, 50p, 20p)	£115.00

Platinum 2007 Coins have recently been issued

2007 Britannia design £25 coin, issue price £495. 2007 Britannia £10 coin, issue price £195

Gold Britannia issues began in 1987, as both bullion issues, as well as proof collectors' issues. The values of the bullion issues are based on the value of the gold content, which fluctuates daily. The prices for these issues are given only as a guideline.

Bullion .917 Gold (UNC) Issues

£10	tenth ounce	Bullion Value + 30 to 50%
£25	quarter ounce	Bullion Value + 12 to 25%
£50	half ounce	Bullion Value + 8 to 20%
£100	one ounce	Bullion Value + 5 to 15%

The following are 4-piece sets, each coin encapsulated, and housed in a clamshell case,.

Special Collectors' (PROOF) sets

1987	10,000	Britannia standing	£900.00
1988	3,505	Britannia standing	£925.00
1989	2,268	Britannia standing	£1000.00
1990	527	Britannia standing	£950.00
1991	509	Britannia standing	£900.00
1992	500	Britannia standing	£900.00
1993	462	Britannia standing	£925.00
1994	435	Britannia standing	£950.00
1995	500	Britannia standing	£1000.00
1996	483	Britannia standing	£1000.00
1997	892	Britannia standing	£1000.00
1998	750	Britannia standing	£1000.00
1999	750	Britannia standing	£1050.00
2000	750	Britannia standing	£1000.00
2001	1,000	Una & the Lion	£900.00
2002	945	Britannia standing	£900.00
2003	1,250	Britannia with Helmet	£900.00
2004	1,250	Britannia standing	£900.00
2005	1,250	Britannia seated	£925.00
2006	1,250	Britannia standing	£1000.00
2007		Britannia seated	£1225.00

Britannia (PROOF) invividual cased coins

£100	1997	£660.00
£100	Other dates	£450.00-£550.00
£50	All dates	£250.00-£300.00
£25	All dates	£100.00-£160.00
£10	All dates	Around £70.00-£100

Gold Sovereign-based single coins are defined as non-commemorative Five Pounds, Two Pounds, Sovereigns and Half Sovereigns struck to normal or proof standards and sold singularly as gold bullion coins or as proof collectors' coins. The non-proof coins do not have boxes or certificates and are normally just traded as gold. Sovereigns and half sovereigns are 22 carat gold (.917 fine) and weigh 7.98g and 3.97g respectively.

Five Pounds

1984	Cased proof only	£600.00
1984	Cased proof only with 'U' in circle next to date	£550.00
1985	Cased proof only	£650.00
1985	with 'U' in circle next to date	£550.00
1986	with 'U' in circle next to date	£550.00
1987	with 'U' in circle next to date	£550.00
1988	with 'U' in circle next to date	£550.00
1989	Sovereign Anniversary type	£600.00
1989	Sovereign Anniversary type, cased proof	£700.00
1990	with 'U' in circle next to date	£580.00
1991	with 'U' in circle next to date	£580.00
1992	with 'U' in circle next to date	£580.00
1993	with 'U' in circle next to date	£580.00
1994	with 'U' in circle next to date	£580.00
1995	with 'U' in circle next to date	£580.00
1996	with 'U' in circle next to date	£580.00
1997	with 'U' in circle next to date	£650.00
1998	New portrait	£650.00
1999		£650.00
2000		£600.00
2000	with 'U' in circle next to date	£600.00
2001		£600.00
2002	Shield reverse	£650.00
2003		£600.00
2004		£600.00
2005		£650.00
2006		£650.00
2007		£740.00

Two Pounds (double sovereign)

All are cased proofs. The £2 coin has not often been issued on its own.

1987		£300.00
1988		£300.00
1989	Sovereign Anniversary type	£350.00
1990		£300.00
1991		£300.00
1992		£300.00
1993		£300.00
1996		£300.00

Sovereigns, loose bullion type

Sovereigns of the 1970s and 1980s are generally traded at their bullion value. They contain 7.32 grammes of fine gold. Particularly perfect examples may be worth a slight premium. The dates struck were as follows:

1974, 1976, 1978, 1979, 1980, 1981 and 1982	Bullion Value

Modern bullion type sovereigns, from 2000 to date, tend to sell for a little more than bullion value. The dates struck were as follows:

2000, 2001, 2002, 2003, 2004, 2005, 2006, 2007	£110.00 to £140.00

Sovereigns, cased proof type

1979		£110.00
1980		£110.00
1981		£110.00
1982		£110.00
1983		£110.00
1984		£120.00
1985		£130.00
1986		£120.00
1987		£120.00
1988		£130.00
1989	500th Anniversary of the Sovereign	£530.00
1990		£160.00
1991		£160.00
1992		£160.00
1993		£160.00
1994		£160.00
1995		£160.00
1996		£160.00
1997		£160.00
1998		£160.00
1999		£160.00
2000		£150.00
2001		£150.00
2002		£150.00
2003		£150.00
2004		£150.00
2005		£165.00
2006		£150.00
2007		£200.00

Half Sovereigns, loose bullion type

Until recently, the 1982 Half Sovereign was the only non-proof coin and continues to trade at approximately bullion value. In 2000 the Royal Mint started issuing non-proof half sovereigns and have done so each year since. The 2000 to 2007 half sovereigns tend to trade from about £65 to £80. The shield reverse 2002 coin and the St. George 2005 coin are the most popular.

Half Sovereigns, cased proof type

1979	£60.00
1980	£60.00
1981	£60.00
1982	£60.00
1983	£60.00
1984	£60.00
1985	£60.00
1986	£60.00
1987	£60.00
1988	£60.00
1989	£100.00
1990	£65.00
1991	£65.00
1992	£70.00
1993	£70.00
1994	£70.00
1995	£70.00
1996	£70.00
1997	£70.00
1998	£70.00
1999	£70.00
2000	£70.00
2001	£70.00
2002	£85.00
2003	£75.00
2004	£75.00
2005	£75.00
2006	£90.00
2007	£100.00

1980	10,000	£5, £2, Sovereign (£1), 1/2 Sovereign	£500.00
1981	-	Set containing 9 coins including silver Crown	£700.00
1982	2,500	£5, £2, Sovereign (£1), 1/2 Sovereign	£700.00
1983		£2, Sovereign (£1), 1/2 Sovereign	£300.00
1984	7,095	£5, Sovereign (£1), 1/2 Sovereign	£550.00
1985	5,849	£5, £2, Sovereign (£1), 1/2 Sovereign	£700.00
1986	12,000	£2 Commonwealth Games, Sovereign (£1), 1/2 Sovereign	£300.00
1987	12,500	£2, Sovereign (£1), 1/2 Sovereign	£325.00
1988	12,500	£2, Sovereign (£1), 1/2 Sovereign	£300.00
1989	5,000	£5, £2, Sovereign (£1), 1/2 Sovereign (Anniversary reverse)	£1600.00
	7,936	£2, Sovereign (£1), 1/2 Sovereign (Anniversary reverse)	£1000.00
1990	1,721	£5, £2, Sovereign (£1), 1/2 Sovereign	£800.00
	1,937	£2, Sovereign (£1), 1/2 Sovereign	£400.00
1991	1,336	£5, £2, Sovereign (£1), 1/2 Sovereign	£800.00
	1,152	£2, Sovereign (£1), 1/2 Sovereign	£400.00
1992	1,165	£5, £2, Sovereign (£1), 1/2 Sovereign	£800.00
	967	£2, Sovereign (£1), 1/2 Sovereign	£400.00
1993	1,078	£5, £2, Sovereign (£1), 1/2 Sovereign (Pistrucci medallion)	£900.00
	663	£2, Sovereign (£1), 1/2 Sovereign	£500.00
1994	918	£5, £2 (Bank of England), Sovereign (£1), 1/2 Sovereign	£900.00
	1,249	£2 (Bank of England), Sovereign (£1), 1/2 Sovereign	£400.00
1995	718	£5, £2 (Dove of Peace), Sovereign (£1), 1/2 Sovereign	£800.00
	1,112	£2 (Dove of Peace), Sovereign (£1), 1/2 Sovereign	£550.00
1996	742	£5, £2, Sovereign (£1), 1/2 Sovereign	£800.00
	868	£2, Sovereign (£1), 1/2 Sovereign	£500.00
1997	860	£5, £2 (bi-metallic), Sovereign (£1), 1/2 Sovereign	£850.00
	817	£2 (bi-metallic), Sovereign (£1), 1/2 Sovereign	£500.00
1998	789	£5, £2, Sovereign (£1), 1/2 Sovereign	£800.00
	560	£2, Sovereign (£1), 1/2 Sovereign	£500.00
1999	991	£5, £2 (Rugby World Cup), Sovereign (£1), 1/2 Sovereign	£1000.00
	912	£2 (Rugby World Cup), Sovereign (£1), 1/2 Sovereign	£650.00
2000	1,000	£5, £2, Sovereign (£1), 1/2 Sovereign	£800.00
	1,250	£2, Sovereign (£1), 1/2 Sovereign	£500.00
2001	1,000	£5, £2 (Marconi), Sovereign (£1), 1/2 Sovereign	£800.00
	891	£2 (Marconi), Sovereign (£1), 1/2 Sovereign	£500.00
2002	3,000	£5, £2, Sovereign (£1), 1/2 Sovereign (Shield reverse)	£1000.00
	3,947	£2, Sovereign (£1), 1/2 Sovereign.(Shield reverse)	£600.00
2003	2,250	£5, £2, Sovereign (£1), 1/2 Sovereign	£800.00
	1,717	£2 (DNA), Sovereign (£1), 1/2 Sovereign	£500.00
2004	2,250	£5, £2, Sovereign (£1), 1/2 Sovereign	£800.00
	2,500	£2, £1 (Forth Bridge), 1/2 Sovereign	£550.00
2005	1,500	£5, £2, Sovereign (£1), 1/2 Sovereign	£950.00
	2,500	£2, Sovereign (£1), 1/2 Sovereign	£500.00
2006	1,750	£5, £2, Sovereign (£1), 1/2 Sovereign	£900.00
2006	1,750	£2, Sovereign (£1), 1/2 Sovereign	£500.00
2007		Sovereign, 1/2 Sovereign	£315.00
2007	700	£2, Sovereign, 1/2 Sovereign	£700.00

Based on a tradition dating back to the 12th century, every year on Maundy Thursday (the day before Good Friday), the monarch distributes leather pouches of special coins to selected people in a Royal Ceremony. The number of recipients is equal to the age of the monarch, as is the value of the coins in each pouch.

All Maundy coinage issued under the reign of Queen Elizabeth II carries the same obverse portrait, that of the first bust of the Queen used on coins and designed by Mary Gillick.

Prices listed here are for complete sets in official Royal Mint cases, which became standard in in the 1960s. Commencing in 1989, the coins are individually encapsulated within the case.

1971	1,018	Tewkesbury Abbey	£90.00
1972	1,026	York Minster	£95.00
1973	1,004	Westminster Abbey	£90.00
1974	1,042	Salisbury Cathedral	£90.00
1975	1,050	Peterborough Cathedral	£90.00
1976	1,158	Hereford Cathedral	£90.00
1977	1,138	Westminster Abbey	£90.00
1978	1,178	Carlisle Cathedral	£90.00
1979	1,188	Winchester Cathedral	£90.00
1980	1,198	Worcester Cathedral	£90.00
1981	1,178	Westminster Abbey	£90.00
1982	1,218	St. David's Cathedral, Dyfed	£90.00
1983	1,228	Exeter Cathedral	£90.00
1984	1,238	Southwell Minster	£90.00
1985	1,248	Ripon Cathedral	£95.00
1986	1,378	Chichester Cathedral	£90.00
1987	1,390	Ely Cathedral	£90.00
1988	1,402	Lichfield Cathedral	£90.00
1989	1,353	Birmingham Cathedral	£90.00
1990	1,523	Newcastle Cathedral	£90.00
1991	1,384	Westminster Abbey	£90.00
1992	1,424	Chester Cathedral	£90.00
1993	1,440	Wells Cathedral	£90.00
1994	1,433	Truro Cathedral	£90.00

1995	1,466	Coventry Cathedral	£90.00
1996	1,629	Norwich Cathedral	£90.00
1997	1,786	Bradford Cathedral	£95.00
1998	1,654	Portsmouth Cathedral	£90.00
1999	1,676	Bristol Cathedral	£90.00
2000	1,684	Lincoln Cathedral	£90.00
2000	13,180	silver proof set, taken from special "Millennium Proof Set" listed on pg. 69	£90.00
2001	1,706	Westminster Abbey	£90.00
2002	1,678	Canterbury Cathedral	£90.00
2002	2,002	gold proof set, taken from special "Golden Jubilee Proof Set" listed on pg. 69	£90.00
2003		Gloucester Cathedral	£90.00
2004		Liverpool (Anglican) Cathedral	£90.00
2005		Wakefield Cathedral	£90.00

INFO

On "Decimalisation Day" in 1971, all Maundy money was re-valuated to decimal pence (the old 1d pieces became worth 1p decimal). Since 1971, the coins have the face value of 1p, 2p, 3p, 4p although there is no significant change in design to note this transition.

Some people are not really into numismatic collectables....

For those of you that are...

CHECK YOUR CHANGE - UK DECIMAL MONEY